The Holocaust

Published by IWM, Lambeth Road, London SE1 6HZ
iwm.org.uk

ISBN 978-1-912423-40-8

A catalogue record for this book is
available from the British Library.
Printed and bound by Printer Trento Srl
Colour reproduction by DL Imaging

Every effort has been made to contact all copyright holders.
The publishers will be glad to make good in future editions
any error or omissions brought to their attention.

A note on the text: This publication uses place names as
they were at the time of the historic moment that is being
described. Many of these names – including those of
countries, towns and cities – have since changed.

Front cover: Railway tracks from the former Platform 17 at
Berlin-Grunewald Station in Germany. This was the platform
the Nazis used to deport tens of thousands of Jewish people
who had been rounded up in Berlin to ghettos and camps in
occupied eastern Europe. Few ever returned.

The Holocaust

JAMES BULGIN

CONTENTS

I want the coming generation to remember our times…
I don't know my fate. I don't know whether I will be
able to tell you what happened later.

Nachum Grzywacz, July 1942

PROLOGUE

Jewish people had, by the early twentieth century, been living in Europe for over 2,000 years. Over this period their experiences developed in highly diverse ways.

At times they were able to flourish, while at others they were persecuted and attacked for their perceived differences. As a minority group, they have been persistently identified as 'outsiders'.

By the 1930s, although they still faced discrimination, Jewish people were recognised as citizens in most European countries, occupying roles in trades, professions and industries across European society.

For historic reasons, the largest numbers of Jewish people lived in eastern Europe – but even here they were a relatively small proportion of the overall population. In central and western Europe, this proportion was even smaller.

This bottle is from the factory of the family-run Haberfeld distillery in Oświęcim, Poland. Liquors from the distillery were well known across the Austro-Hungarian Empire. Founded in 1804, it was the town's largest business by the early 1900s. Alfons Haberfeld, who ran the company in the 1930s, was also the leader of the local Jewish community.

The Wohl Family ∨

Leonhard Wohl was born in 1886 and raised in Bublitz, a small town in northern Germany. He was the seventh of ten children. Together with his older brother Alex, he took over the family corn-merchant business. Leonhard married Erna in 1910 and they had two daughters. Tragically, Erna died a year after the birth of their second child. Leonhard married again and had two more daughters with his second wife, Clara. Leonhard spoilt his daughters and they loved his sense of humour.

Below: Leonhard Wohl in First World War uniform; Leonhard Wohl and two soldiers during the First World War.

The Lasker Family ∧

Anita Lasker was born in 1925. She lived with her parents Edith and Alfons and two older sisters Marianne and Renate in Breslau, Germany. Anita's mother was an excellent violinist and encouraged all three of her children to play a musical instrument from a young age — Anita took up the cello. The family regularly played chess, inspired by Anita's uncle Edward who was a world-class chess player. On Sundays they only spoke French while at home to help learn the language.

Top: Anita *(right)* with her two sisters Marianne and Renate; Alfons and Edith Lasker sitting on the grass; Alfons on the ice with his three daughters.

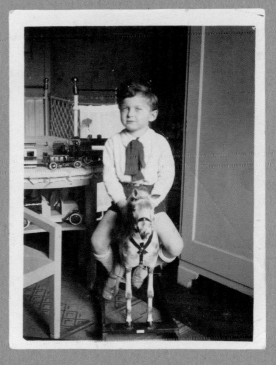

The Imich Family

Stanisław Imich came from a prosperous family in Częstochowa, Poland. He served in the Polish Army during the Polish–Soviet War (1919–1921) before studying medicine and becoming a doctor. In 1920 he married Anna Gumplowicz, who was from a well-known Kraków family, and set up home with her in the city. He specialised in the use of X-rays and spent time away working in Vienna. In 1930 Stanisław and Anna had a son, Jan.

Clockwise from top left: Jan Imich feeds pigeons with his grandfather Jósef in Kraków, Poland; Jan Imich skiing on holiday; Jan Imich as a child on a rocking horse; Stanisław and Anna Imich with their son Jan.

Above: Group outside a public kitchen in Nowogródek, Poland. The majority of people living in Nowogródek had been Jewish for generations, but at the start of the 1900s ongoing economic problems meant that many of them sought to emigrate to the US (United States of America), seeking better lives.

Right: Members of the Jewish community in Salonika, Greece on the Sabbath, May 1916.

Alfred 'Freddie' Knoller was born in 1921 and lived in Vienna with his family.

Below: An informal portrait of the Knoller family in the 1920s. Freddie — in the middle — was the youngest son.

The Heidenfeld Family ⌃

Georg Heidenfeld was a doctor who served as a medical officer in the German Army during the First World War. He lived in Kanth, near Breslau, with his wife Stefanie and two daughters, Hortense and Beate. His practice was based in the family's large home.

Above: Hortense and Beate Heidenfeld with a dog.
Bottom right: Georg and Stefanie Heidenfeld.

The Hajdu Family ›

János Hajdu was born to György and Livia in Budapest in 1937. The family lived in a predominantly Jewish part of the city.

Top right: György Hajdu poses for a studio portrait with his mother Ida in Budapest, Hungary.
Bottom right: János Hajdu and a teddy bear.

The Trompeter Family ^

Tauba Trompeter *(far right)* was born into an Orthodox Jewish family in Mielec, Poland. She had four sisters and two brothers. Her father, Jacob Isaac, was a local grain-trader while her mother Gitla ran a small general store from their home. At home Tauba spoke Yiddish and at school she spoke Polish. Many of her relatives lived in the US and in Germany, having left Poland to seek better lives after the First World War.

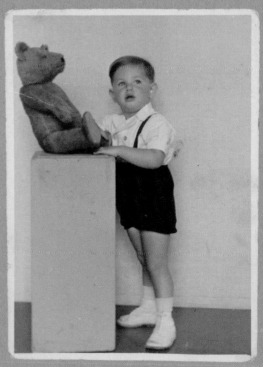

The Asscher Family >

Dolf Asscher was born in the Netherlands in 1931 to William and Roosje. His father was an engineer and the family had a long history in medicine and law as well as art and literature.

Right: Dolf Asscher as a baby in his highchair.

Oswald Jacobi ⌄

Oswald Jacobi was born to Else and Fritz on 17 September 1922. His *brit milah* (circumcision ceremony) took place on the second day of *Rosh Hashanah* (Jewish New Year), which was said by his rabbi to be a special *mitzvah* (commandment). His parents, who were concerned about the turmoil in Germany after the First World War, gave him the middle name Herbert to use if he ever needed to leave for an English-speaking country.

Below: Oswald Jacobi grew up in Frankfurt, Germany.

The Felix Family ^

Kitty Felix was born in 1926, five years after her brother Robert. They lived with their parents in the town of Bielsko in Poland.

Above: Kitty and Robert Felix, 1939; The Felix family.

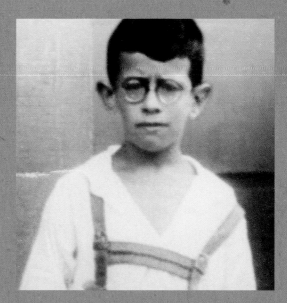

The Siegel Family

Michael Siegel was a highly respected lawyer in Munich. He lived in the city with his wife Mathilde and two children.

This page, clockwise from top: The Siegels skiing in fancy dress with friends; Bea Siegel and her brother Peter playing outside; Bea Siegel *(front row, third from left)* with her *Kindergarten* class dressed up for *Fasching,* a Bavarian carnival.

Opposite, clockwise from top left: Bea Siegel, her brother and mother; the Siegel family in front of a souvenir shop; the Siegel family sitting outside.

CHAPTER ONE

Old Empires and New Nation States

At the start of the twentieth century European empires continued to dominate the globe – but the balance of power was shifting.

National independence movements were putting increasing pressure on imperial control, threatening the stability of empires from within their own borders. The nationalisms that drove those within these movements were given renewed focus – and an accompanying sense of implied legitimacy – by authors who adapted theories developed by Darwin to popularise the idea of racial superiority. The new science of eugenics argued that the 'weak' were outbreeding the 'strong', thanks to the 'unnatural' comforts afforded by modern civilisation. 'Social Darwinists' spread the idea that life was a struggle for survival – a notion that received backing especially among European colonial powers.

The outbreak of the First World War in 1914 became the catalyst for foundational change. Catastrophic violence was unleashed on an unprecedented scale, shattering the illusion of civilisation that had sustained generations of Western attitudes, assumptions and outlooks. Apart from the loss of life (which was unparalleled at the time), the war saw the creation of huge prisoner of war camps – and the new reality of refugee camps – on European soil.

9·Nov·1918

Arma judaica Germanorum

The Russian Empire, which collapsed following the revolution in 1917, was the first of four empires to fall. The German and Austro-Hungarian Empires came to an end shortly afterwards as they were deconstructed in the peace deal that ended the war. The Ottoman Empire followed in 1922. From these former empires, new nation states emerged. These 'successor states' came to be defined not just by geographic borders, but by 'ethnic identity' too – a concept known as

'ethno-nationalism'. Within these nations, nationalisms developed a renewed intensity, igniting border wars, tensions and extremist politics.

Ideas about biological destiny and assumptions about certain population groups being 'out of place' took hold. In this volatile context, pre-war arguments about eugenics gained new impetus and focus. The notion that certain population groups were 'out of place' in a world of emerging nation-states grew and the concepts of 'superfluous peoples' and statelessness became realities. It became clear that the end of the First World War had merely set the stage for new forms of division and conflict.

Martin Bormann

Martin Bormann joined the German Army in June 1918, but never saw active service in the First World War. After being discharged he worked in agriculture, becoming the estate manager of a farm. In 1922 he joined the *Freikorps*, a nationalist paramilitary group. Two years later he was jailed for his role in a politically motivated murder. After his release, he became a member of the Nazi Party. In 1933 he was promoted to be chief of staff to Deputy *Führer* Rudolf Hess.

Adolf Hitler

Hitler's early years of adulthood were spent pursuing an unsuccessful career as an artist in Vienna. Service in the First World War changed his life, however, giving his aimless existence a new sense of purpose and direction. Radicalised by the shock of defeat, he became convinced that Jews had conspired to ensure Germany's downfall. These ideas were first introduced to him by soldiers he was convalescing with after being injured during the war. After the war he was sent to spy on a Nazi meeting, but became enraptured by the message of the movement — by 1921 he had become the leader of the Nazi Party. In 1923 Hitler led an ill-fated attempt to overthrow the government which became known as the Munich Putsch. He planned to take control of the Bavarian state government and then march on Berlin. The uprising was quickly suppressed and Hitler was arrested. He was sentenced to five years in prison for treason, but was released after just eight months.

Fighting for Power

The end of the First World War in November 1918 left Germany in chaos. Most Germans felt widespread anger at their country's surrender, blaming their defeat not on the military commanders, but on the 'November criminals' in the government. Under the tenets of this conspiratorial belief, they were convinced that they had been 'stabbed in the back' by an unseen enemy within. Increasing numbers of Germans began claiming that 'the Jews' were at the centre of this and were responsible for their nation's humiliation. With the war lost, and facing revolution at home, Germany's political leaders had no choice but to sign the Treaty of Versailles in June 1919. The terms of the Treaty caused widespread outrage among Germans. It forced Germany to disarm, pay reparations and surrender territory – and it held Germany responsible for starting the war.

Opposite: Words and images became weapons in a violent political struggle. Posters were important campaigning tools. They bombarded voters with eye-catching symbols and powerful slogans that appealed to people's fears and desires. In the crucial elections of 1932, the Nazis produced more propaganda than any other political party.

Clockwise from top left: Propaganda poster, *Rettet die Deutsche Familie* (Save the German family); Propaganda poster, *Arbeiter der Stirn der Faust Wählt den Frontsoldaten Hitler!* (Workers who work with the head or the fist, vote for the soldier who served at the front – Hitler!); Propaganda poster, *Unsere Letzte Hoffnung: Hitler* (Our last hope: Hitler); Propaganda poster, *Hitler*.

Rettet die deutsche Familie

Wählt
National-
Sozialisten

Liste 8

ARBEITER

DER STIRN
DER FAUST

WÄHLT DEN FRONTSOLDATEN

HITLER!

HiTLER

Unsere
letzte
Hoffnung:

HITLER

Joseph Goebbels

Joseph Goebbels was rejected for military service during the First World War because of a club foot. He concentrated instead on his academic studies and received a doctorate in German philosophy and literature in 1921. He was trying to make a living as a writer when he joined the Nazi Party. Goebbels understood the media's power to shape public opinion and the appeal of violence as a recruitment tool. After successfully organising Nazi election campaigns, he was promoted to Reich Minister of Propaganda in March 1933.

Alfred Rosenberg

Alfred Rosenberg was one of the Nazi Party's longest-standing members, joining the movement much earlier than other senior figures. He was an obsessive antisemite and conspiracy theorist, believing that Jews were plotting world domination. Rosenberg was given temporary command of the Party during Hitler's imprisonment but under his leadership it descended into chaos. Rosenberg thought of himself as the Nazis' philosopher and leading race theorist – his influential book *The Myth of the Twentieth Century* outlined many of the Nazis' racial ideologies.

Opposite: In Grösster Not Wählte Hindenburg Adolf Hitler zum Reichskanzler (In a time of the greatest necessity Hindenburg elected Adolf Hitler as Reich Chancellor). The Nazis promoted the partnership between President Hindenburg and the newly appointed chancellor as a union between the conservative politics of war-hero Hindenburg and the new, dynamic style of Hitler and the Nazis.

A new democracy – the Weimar Republic – governed post-war Germany, replacing the imperial rule of the Kaisers. The leaders of this Republic struggled to cope with mass unemployment and continued food shortages. Extremist political parties on the left and right sought to exploit these problems and to challenge its very existence in an attempt to replace it with radical alternatives. Violence became a central part of German politics as these parties created private armies and fought each other. Voter intimidation, brawls and assassinations became increasingly commonplace as political argument was expressed through fists and weapons alongside rhetoric. The situation worsened when attempts by the government to address missed payments for war reparations by printing money led to spiralling inflation in the early 1920s. The hyperinflation that followed ravaged Germany's fragile economy and devastated the livelihoods and savings of many of its citizens.

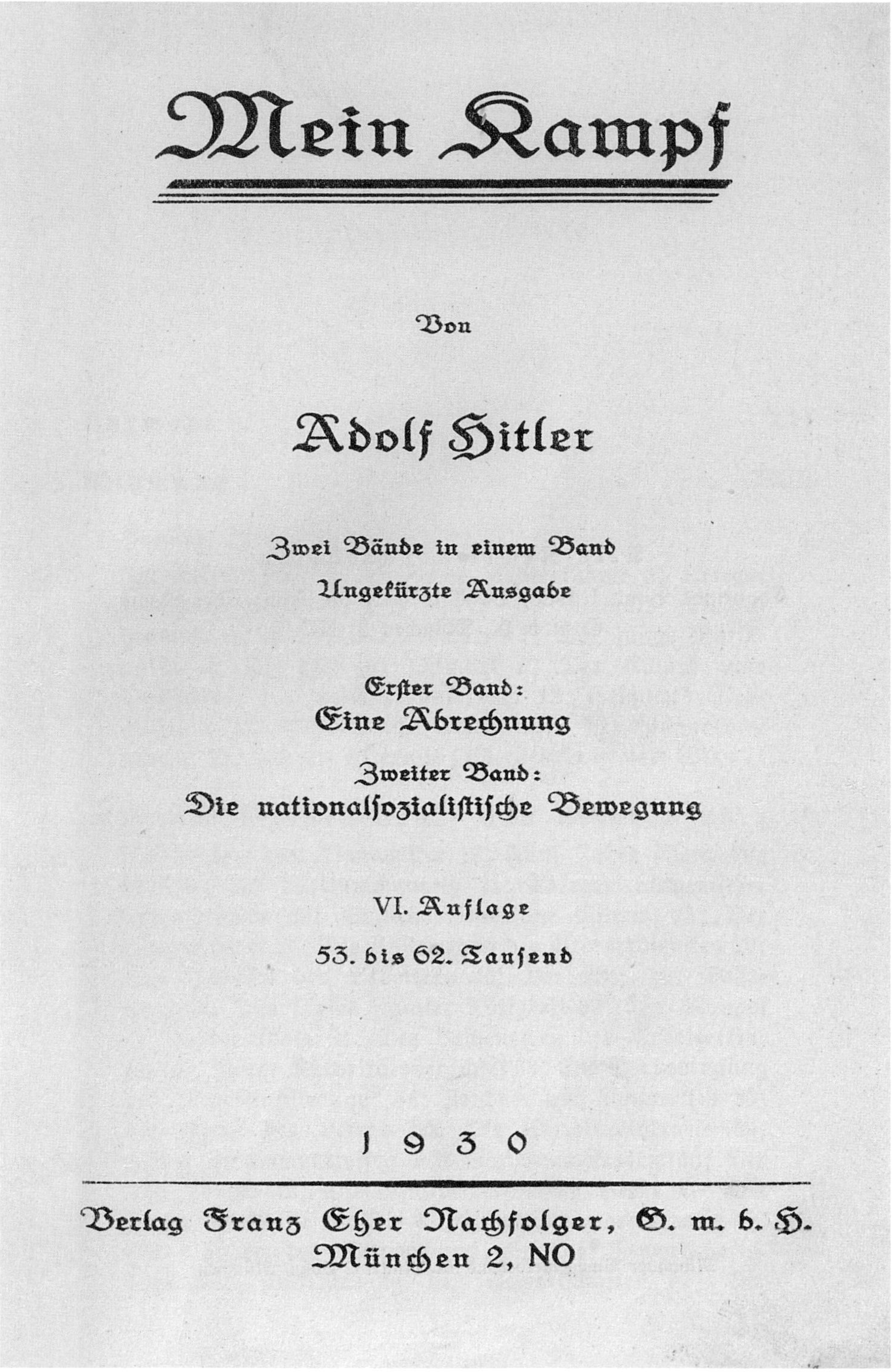

Mein Kampf

Von

Adolf Hitler

Zwei Bände in einem Band
Ungekürzte Ausgabe

Erster Band:
Eine Abrechnung

Zweiter Band:
Die nationalsozialistische Bewegung

VI. Auflage
53. bis 62. Tausend

1 9 3 0

Verlag Franz Eher Nachfolger, G. m. b. H.
München 2, NO

Heinrich Himmler

Heinrich Himmler was desperate to fight in the First World War, but it ended before he was able to do so. He received a degree in agriculture in 1922 and joined the Nazi Party the following year. He quickly developed a reputation as a skilled organiser and facilitator. In 1929 he was given control of Hitler's bodyguards, the *Schutzstaffel* (SS) — whose numbers were very small at this stage. Himmler was a staunch believer in 'blood and soil' — the idea that German strength came from racial purity, with its roots in the countryside.

Opposite: While in prison for his role in the 1923 Munich Putsch, Hitler began work on *Mein Kampf* (*My Struggle*). It became the most important written work of the Nazi movement. Both a memoir and a manifesto, it gave violent expression to Hitler's hatred of Jews and communism and laid out his vision for a racially pure Germany.

In the political upheaval, a small right-wing group called the *Nationalsozialistische Deutsche Arbeiterpartei* (National Socialist German Workers' Party) emerged, alongside many other dissident fringe groups. In time they would become better known as the 'Nazis'. Their leader Adolf Hitler claimed to have the answers to Germany's problems, promising a national rebirth and a return of status and prosperity for both the country and its citizens. His claims for Germany's future were contingent on the destruction of his enemies, both real and imagined. The main focus of his hatred was communists and Jews – though he routinely conflated these two groups.

By the mid-1920s, Germany had begun to stabilise, allowing moderate democratic parties to gain a foothold. As this continued, the appeal of radical politics declined. This recovery was fragile, however, and would rely on a period of economic stability to succeed. Hopes for such stability were rapidly undone in 1929 by the crash of the New York stock market. The turmoil in America sparked a global financial crisis. Loans that had underpinned Germany's improving situation during the 1920s were recalled, toppling its economy into disaster and creating deprivation and devastating hardship for people across the country. The ruling moderate government collapsed.

In these chaotic new circumstances, growing numbers of Germans were drawn to Hitler's vague promises of revival. Public resentment towards the chaos in Germany made the promise of strong leadership and order that he claimed to

Hermann Göring

Hermann Göring became famous as a fighter pilot during the First World War. His celebrity and his links to the German aristocracy made him valuable to Hitler. He joined the Nazis in 1922 and was seriously injured during the attempted *Putsch* (coup) in 1923. He fled the country to avoid arrest and to recover, returning to Germany in 1927. Göring became a member of the cabinet when Hitler was appointed chancellor. He was given sweeping powers over the police and surveillance in Prussia, Germany's largest state.

offer appealing. His party had been forced on to the political fringes as their support diminished in tandem with the country's stabilisation. However, the upheaval that followed the crash reversed this trend. Their following grew rapidly, taking them from relative obscurity towards the centre of power.

Votes for the Nazis grew in 1930 – in the first of a series of elections – before reaching their peak in 1932. In the same year, Hitler mounted a bid to win election as president of Germany. He was narrowly defeated by the incumbent, war hero Field Marshal Paul von Hindenburg, but Hitler's passionate, countrywide electioneering won him significant admiration and support. By 1932, the Nazis had become the largest party in parliament. They were unable to secure enough votes to claim a majority but had become a major parliamentary voice.

Established politicians worried that Hitler could be dangerous but did not know how to control him. Recognising that his levels of support would need to be acknowledged, they began to think that if he was chancellor he would be easier to control and his popularity could be harnessed. Advisors to the President of Germany, Paul von Hindenburg, shared the Nazis' hatred and mistrust of the left-wing German Communist Party (KPD) and the Social Democratic Party (SPD) and wanted to use Hitler to destroy their common enemies. In the early weeks of 1933, they convinced the reluctant president to appoint him, and on 30 January Hitler was named as chancellor of Germany. Those who counselled Hindenburg believed that

Opposite: Eighteen-year-old Gerda Cimbal wrote this letter to her English pen pal Mollie McEvoy at the height of the Nazi struggle for power. It reflects the anxieties felt by Germans at the time, including unemployment. Gerda writes that she is hopeful she will be able to find work because she is so young.

Berlin, den 13. Jan. 1933.

My dear Mollie,

I was very glad to receive your letter. I think you celebrate Christmas in another way than we in Germany. Did you have mistletoe and holly-tree? I learned so.

On Christmas we do not make so many dances and carnevals. The 2nd holyday I went with my mother in the forest near Berlin. Here on a frozen lake people was skating while the weather was rather warm and the sun shone. I have also skates and high shoes but this winter I had no time to skate.

At school we have very much to do. We learn already the writing of a letter, of suing a situation. Do you understand, what I mean?

I thank you very much for correcting my mistakes and I am very ashamed to make so badone. No, dear Mollie, your English is not too difficult for me; I can it understand very well.

Enclosed you find a piece of a newspaper with some advertisements. Here you can see what our cinemas are playing. Harris "Unter den" is the most famous coffee-house in Berlin. Have you anybody, who can explain you the pronounciation of German? It is very difficult to declare that in a letter. But I will tell you the pronounciation of days-name as well as possible.

Montag say 'o' like in 'no' and 'a' like 'but'
Dienstag — Dienstag "
Mittwoch — Mittwoch I can not explain you this etc.
Donnerstag — otherwise
Freitag — Frytag
Sonnabend — 'a' like 'u' in gun, 'i' like 'i' in 'it'
Sonntag —

Do you live near London? I think in Lancashire there are many mines and a big export of coal. Is it not? We have in Silesia and near the Rhine also large coal mines. Here you sea a picture of an orchard near my home. Often I wish to go there but now it is impossible. First I have to earn money. Do you need a type-writer or a book-keeper in your farm? You know I am seeking a situation.

Now I will give you a distribtion of my face. I have light-red cheeks, grey-blue eyes and light-brown hair. I am 6 time as tall as this letter-paper. I suppose that is a very funny discription. I cannot see much of your face on your photograph. I must imagine.

Please tell me something of your life at school, your teachers and friends. Do you have in your town men ill of influence (gippe) tek in London?

I cannot imagine to have a king in the land. We have only our President the imperial diet with the delegates. Then there are the many parties. On our last choice we had 38 parties. But the motion of Adolf Hitler is the largest. Do you hear sometimes of him?

I have read from the burned French ship "L'Atlantique". This a disease.

This time I have no stamps to send you but on the envelope yours will find different stamps. I give your stamps to the girls of my class who are very glad to receive them. In your former letters you paid 5 Halfpence and in the last only 3 Halfpence. What is that?

Please answer soonly.

With my very best love I am Your friend

Gerda.

Private Armies

The *Sturmabteilung* (known as the SA) was the Nazis' paramilitary wing. Its members marched through Germany's streets, intimidating and attacking political enemies. Nazi leaders saw the organisation as the embodiment of the strength and determination of their movement. The SA's distinctive brown uniform earned its members the nickname 'brownshirts' and set it apart from other armed groups. The shirt, breeches and marching boots were all modelled on military designs. The SA offered unemployed, disillusioned young men and veterans an opportunity to channel their anger and aggression.

By 1932, the SA had more than 400,000 members — four times that of the German Army. It was organised into regional groups. These were distinguished by the colour of their collar patches and later the bands around their cap. Across Germany the SA was responsible for protecting Nazi political meetings and disrupting those of their opponents.

Above left: SA cap.

once Hitler was in a position of power and authority, the violence of his rhetoric and ideology would be tempered. It was a catastrophic mistake, which ultimately only served to give Hitler the opening that he needed.

Shortly after Hitler's appointment as chancellor, the German parliament building, the Reichstag, was badly damaged in an arson attack. Hitler seized this as an opportunity to expand his power, blaming the communists and introducing laws that allowed them to be imprisoned without trial. In the days that followed, thousands of Hitler's political opponents were beaten, arrested and effectively pressured into silence. Despite these violent political tactics, the Nazis failed to win an overall majority in the March 1933 elections. In order to secure the control they wanted, Hitler forced through the 'Enabling Act' later the same month. This transferred law-making powers from parliament to Hitler's cabinet and allowed him to establish what was in effect a dictatorship. By mid-July the Nazis were the only political party in Germany.

Although Hitler's powers were wide-ranging, his authority was still technically held in check by President Hindenburg. As president, Hindenburg was in theory still able to limit Hitler's power by preventing him from determining policy autonomously. He could even remove him from office. When Hindenburg died in 1934, this obstacle was gone and Hitler took the opportunity to take total control of the Reich. He abolished the office of president and claimed its powers for himself, assuming the title of *Führer* (Leader).

CHAPTER TWO

A New Order

Opposite: As the insignia on this judge's robe suggests, the Nazis did not feel that the law should be impartial. They wanted the legal system to be part of their network of enforcement. Many judges were sympathetic to the views of the Nazis and fell willingly into line with the regime.

O nce in power, the Nazis sought radically to reshape Germany to conform to their world view. Mystical ideas about racial difference were fundamental to the way they understood the world. They believed that all of humanity was driven by a permanent struggle between different groups, or races. For them, some were destined to rule, some were destined to serve and some were destined to be eradicated. This struggle would engender a sense of common purpose, which would require total dedication and commitment from all those who were part of the movement. In Hitler's Germany, the needs of the people would matter more than the needs of the individual. People with the right beliefs, behaviour and biological characteristics would be united into the *Volksgemeinschaft* (people's community), which would be bonded as if it were a single body, with every man, woman and child having their part to play. Those excluded would have no place at all.

As time went on, the more the Nazis became fixated upon who was part of their new community, the more they obsessed about who was not. With their growing power, they used laws, media and culture to impose their ideological vision – and developed an apparatus of terror to enforce it. The messaging used to develop this new society was cultivated and shaped by Hitler and his propaganda minister, Joseph Goebbels. Goebbels carefully managed the public face of the Nazi movement, using a combination of symbols, rituals and mass participation. He ruthlessly mobilised the power of the media to mould Hitler's image.

ADOLF HITLER
Wenn an der Front die Besten fielen, dann könnte man zu Hause wenigstens das Ungeziefer vertilgen, die verräterischen Burschen aus dem Versteck holen und an den höchsten Galgen hängen.

ADOLF HITLER
Der gesunde Mensch mit festem Charakter ist für die Volksgemeinschaft wertvoller als ein geistreicher Schwächling.

ADOLF HITLER
Mögen Jahrtausende vergehen, so wird man nie von Heldentum reden dürfen, ohne des deutschen Heeres des Weltkrieges zu gedenken.

In an early sign of their public hostility towards Jews, the Nazis staged a nationwide boycott of Jewish-owned businesses on 1 April 1933. The SA and Nazi supporters fixed notices with menacing slogans such as 'You bought from Jews! We are watching!' and 'Germans defend yourselves against Jewish atrocity propaganda, buy only at German shops!' to advertise the event. Armed SA men stood guard outside shops to intimidate shoppers. The boycott was originally supposed to last for a full week but was cut short to just one day following international criticism. Adherence to the boycott was mixed. Some shoppers avoided the guards on the main doors by using rear entrances to access retailers and make their purchases, while others were bemused at the intrusion into their lives. Notwithstanding any of this, the early Nazi attempt to deprive Jews of their livelihoods was a sobering signal of intent.

A Cultural Revolution

As part of the effort to guarantee the total Nazification of Germany, Hitler and his party attempted to ensure all political, social and cultural activities furthered their ideological goals. They took control of education, the economy and the law,

Above: Der Führer Spricht (*The Leader Speaks*) was a series of posed images taken by Hitler's official photographer, Heinrich Hoffmann. They presented Hitler as he wished to be seen – as a gifted and passionate speaker. With dramatic gestures building to a frenzied climax, his precisely choreographed speeches became a key part of his appeal.

Opposite top: The Nazis presented Hitler as Germany's saviour, developing a cult of personality around him. *Deutschland Erwacht* (*Germany Awakes*) contained 150 pages with more than 225 images that people could collect and add to the album.

Opposite bottom: These badges are souvenirs from the KdF (*Kraft durch Freude*, meaning 'strength through joy'), a Nazi organisation that provided leisure activities and package holidays for German workers. The badges publicised participation in the national community to other citizens.

Der Kanzler in Neuschwanstein, 1933

Die kleine Gratulantin

Die Jüngsten begrüßen ihren Führer.
Neben ihm sein Adjutant Oberleutnant Brückner

Ein Blumenstrauß aus Kinderhand

138

daß er überall, wo er erkannt wurde, Freude und Beglückung um sich verbreitete.

Die Taschen vollgestopft mit Zigarettenschachteln und Marzipanstücken, so trat er seine Reisen an. Kein Handwerksbursche auf der Straße, der unbeschenkt bleibt. Für jede Mutter ein freundliches Wort, und für jedes Kind einen warmen Händedruck. Nicht umsonst hängt ihm die deutsche Jugend mit ganzer Inbrunst an, denn sie weiß, daß ihr Führer jung ist und daß ihr Wohl und Wehe bei ihm in guten Händen liegt.

Ein Tyrann, der selbstherrlich über seine Satrapen herrscht, so hat ihn die gegnerische marxistische Presse Adolf Hitler gezeichnet. Und wie ist er in Wirklichkeit? Der beste Freund seiner Kameraden. Einer, der für jedes Leid und für jede Not ein weites Herz und menschliches Verständnis hat.

Für den, der Hitler nicht kennt, ist es wie ein Wunder, daß Millionen Menschen ihm so in Liebe und Anhänglichkeit zugetan sind. Für den, der ihn kennt, ist das fast selbstverständlich. In dem unbeschreiblichen Zauber seiner Persönlichkeit liegt das Geheimnis seiner Wirkung. Am meisten wird er von denen geliebt und verehrt, die ihm am innigsten verbunden sind. Und wer ihm einmal die Hand zum Treueschwur reichte, der ist ihm mit Leib und Seele verfallen.

Adolf Hitler hat Deutschland aus seiner tiefsten Erniedrigung wieder zu Ehre und Geltung emporgeführt. Hinter ihm steht eine geschlossene und treue Kämpferschar, die bereit ist, für ihn und seine Idee das Leben hinzugeben. Millionen der besten Deutschen halten ihrem Retter und Führer auf offenen Händen im Bekenntnis zur nationalsozialistischen Volksgemeinschaft ihre Herzen dank.

Ihr schönster Tag

Hitlermädels begrüßen den Führer anläßlich der Wahlreise im Odenwald, 1932

Adolf Hitler inmitten seiner Oberlandler

139

ultimately bringing every organisation in every part of the country under their direct supervision in a process they called *Gleichschaltung*. Over time they passed laws restricting employment for anyone they considered racial enemies or politically suspect and banned trade unions and all types of formal resistance.

The Nazis considered any form of artistic expression to be an integral part of the national community, instigating a realignment of all related activities across Germany. They promised a return to traditional German values, but only as they defined them. Any work created by Jewish artists was rejected.

In a particularly visible act of cultural revolution and destruction, on 10 May 1933 students ransacked libraries for books they considered 'un-German'. They burned works by Jewish, left-wing and liberal authors in public ceremonies across Germany. Books by authors critical of Nazism were also targeted. These organised and co-ordinated events were ritualistic spectacles, in which the participants wielded flaming torches and chanted a series of specially created 'fire oaths' as they thronged around the burning pyres. For those participating, this destruction of culture was a necessary stage in the rebuilding of Germany's future and the redefining of the country's national narrative.

Below left: The Nazis used new technologies to extend the reach of the regime's voice. They helped people buy radios by making models like the *Volksempfänger* (people's radio) more affordable. To encourage communal listening, they also installed radios in public spaces, such as schools and workplaces.

Below right: The *Winterhilfswerk* (Winter Relief Fund) encouraged Germans to support members of the *Volk* (the people) in need. On the annual 'Day of National Solidarity', thousands of people took to the streets with collection tins to gather donations. Those considered enemies of the *Volk*, including Jews, were not entitled to any of this support. Compulsory contributions taken out of wages and social pressure to participate led to people resenting the scheme.

Opposite: Students give the Nazi salute during a book burning, 10 May 1933.

Thinking with the Blood

The Nazis' world-view was rooted in their beliefs about biology.
For them, Germany's destiny relied first and foremost on the
blood that ran through the veins of its people. They thought
that some people were born as super-humans and others as
sub-humans. Jews were considered to be a polluting counter-
race and not really human at all. The Nazis tried to justify these
mystical ideas using scientific arguments, funding research in
the hope that scientists would discover proof for their theories.
Many of the scientists in receipt of these grants knew that the
ideas being proposed were ridiculous, but were prepared to

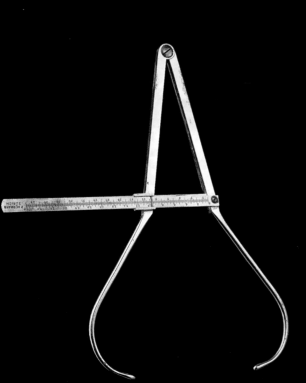

Opposite top: Law for the
Prevention of Hereditarily
Diseased Offspring. In
practice the Nazis' policies
were not based on science,
but on what they believed
to be true. In the end, none
of the scientists the Nazis
commissioned to research
their nonsensical theories
were able to find evidence
to substantiate their beliefs.
Undeterred, the Nazis simply
looked for other forms of
legitimisation.

Opposite bottom left: 'Race
scientists' used instruments
such as these calipers to
measure skull diameter and
nose width. They believed
they could use these
physical characteristics to
classify people into racial
groups. They ranked these
groups in hierarchies
based on their own racist
assumptions.

Opposite bottom right: Nazi
race scientists used this
bust to see if a person's skull
dimensions matched their
Aryan ideal. Historically, the
word 'Aryan' had multiple
meanings. For the Nazis, it
referred to a white European
'master race' in Germany
and Scandinavia – tall,
strong and fair-skinned, with
blonde hair and blue eyes.
Race scientists believed that
physical appearance was a
reflection of racial purity.

accept the money in order to allow them to pursue other work that they were genuinely interested in.

Nazi thinking on race and biology was strongly influenced by ideas about eugenics. Eugenics was the theory that society could be improved by controlling human reproduction. It suggested that social problems had biological solutions and was popular in Europe and the United States. In Germany, it was called *Rassenhygiene* (race hygiene). The movement was founded in the United Kingdom by Sir Francis Galton, whose book *Hereditary Genius*, published in 1869, argued that both mental and physical characteristics were inherited in the same way. Inspired by his cousin Charles Darwin, Galton believed that humans could be selectively bred to improve the species. In the United States, 'race scientists' were alarmed by what they saw as the decline of American 'racial stock'. They blamed this on an influx of immigrants from eastern and southern Europe, as well as relationships between black and white Americans. They advocated laws banning interracial marriages. By the early years of the 1900s there was mounting evidence to discredit such ideas, but the First World War helped revive them, particularly among Germans.

By building on pre-existing thought, the Nazis' ultimate objective was to ensure traits they considered desirable were preserved, while others were eliminated. As part of their determination to create a nation aligned with their ideas about race and genetics, they commissioned scientists to collect data and compile registers identifying 'harmful influences'. People who were considered threats to the health of the national community were targeted with increasingly radical methods. The 1933 'Law for the Prevention of Hereditarily Diseased Offspring' legalised the forced sterilisation of people diagnosed with certain conditions. These included epilepsy, blindness, deafness and mental illness. The most common diagnosis among the 300,000 Germans sterilised was 'feeble-mindedness', a general term that was used to refer to many forms of intellectual disability. The law also allowed for the sterilisation of alleged alcoholics.

Roma Life in Europe

The Romani people, or Roma, have lived in Europe for centuries. They are a diverse community made up of many groups.

Groups in the community share traditions but have different identities. These identities are shaped by their histories, occupations and language. Groups include the Sinti, Lovari, Kalderdash, Kalé, Gitano and Lalleri.

By the 1930s, although some Roma still travelled, the majority across Europe lived settled lives. Sometimes this was by choice and sometimes it was in response to state-imposed restrictions. They adopted the religion and language of the country they lived in and worked in a range of different occupations.

Roma are sometimes referred to as 'Gypsies' in English. This term arose from the belief of the majority of society that the first Roma migrated from Egypt. Although some Roma are proud to describe themselves as 'Gypsies', others find it offensive, believing it suggests negative stereotypes.

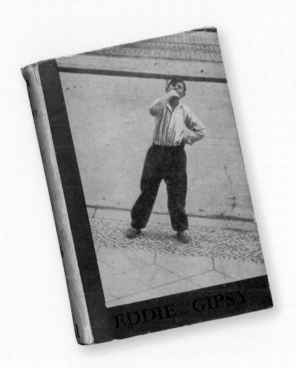

Above left: This is the English-language edition of the German children's book *Ede und Unku*. The popular novel tells the story of the friendship between Ede (Eddie), a working-class German boy, and Unku Lauenburger, a German-Sinti girl. Through the story, Unku challenges common prejudices about Roma that Ede holds. The book includes real-life photographs of the two children.

Indoctrination of Youth

Hitler conceived of his new Germany as the foundation of a 'Third Reich'. In this formulation, the first Reich was Charlemagne's and the second was Bismarck's. Hitler claimed that his radical new Reich would last for a thousand years.

Unku Lauenburger

Unku Lauenburger, a German-Sinti girl, lived with her mother, grandparents and uncle in Berlin. Her parents, Turant and Karl, separated when she was young. She grew up in a green caravan on the same campsite as many of her relatives. The men in her family were musicians and horse traders. Her mother sold lace doilies and sewing items. To earn their living, the extended family travelled to various German towns and cities in the summer but returned to Berlin in the winter.

Below: Nazi children's books taught values of obedience and conformity and told stories about the movement's heroes and history. Some, like *Trust No Fox on the Green Heath and No Jew on his Oath*, introduced children to antisemitic stereotypes of Jews as bullies, cheats and predators. It was written by 18-year-old Elvira Bauer.

To achieve this, he knew that the Nazis needed to indoctrinate children into their world-view from an early age. German boys and girls were exposed to Nazism in the books they read, the films they watched, the clubs they joined and the schools they attended. Millions of the country's youngest citizens enrolled in youth organisations, where they swore a personal oath of allegiance to Hitler.

Werner Holmann
Leipzig · 1045
Brunnenweg 6.

Leipzig, d. 9. Jan 1939

Dear Howard!

I have got your letter by best healthy. I have also got a very beautiful christmas. My presents are: a pullover, a pair of spats, a wrist watch, a ring, a tie and many other thanks.

I have a friend which will work with your friend. Have you still more addresses? Please send them to me.

What you was writing above the Jews is not right. The Jews lives in our country like guests. We does not do them anything. But they had take us away our independent way of thinking and had infested our race. Therefore we don't like them.

Ich habe die Beilagen, die in deinem Briefe waren, erhalten. Ich danke dir für die Marken und für das Andenken an die Ballonpost. Wir sprechen jetzt im Aufsatzlehrgang davon.

Einige andere Verse schreibe ich dir ans Ende dieses Briefes.

Ich schicke dir dann noch einige Rezepte von einer deutschen Firma für das Abkochen im Freien. Zeitungsausschnitte sende ich dir gesondert nach.

Ich will dir nun erzählen wie ich Weihnachten verbracht habe. Früh um 6 Uhr wurden wir durch einen Trommler geweckt. Dann ging es so schnell wie möglich in die gute Stube, wo unsere Geschenke lagen. Ich packte nun auch meine Geschenke aus. Dann wurde der Weihnachtskuchen gekostet. Jetzt betrachteten wir unsere Geschenke genauer. Nach dem Mittagessen gingen wir zu Verwandten um sie zu Weihnachten zu gratulieren. Am 2. Feiertag waren wir hangen.

Aus Neue Jahr haben wir fast 1½ Tag gefeiert.
In einer Anzeige von einem Kino ist der Name Freudel Park erwähnt. Das ist unsere Shirley Temple.

Ich bin jetzt in der Reifeprüfung unserer Schule.

Nun schreibe ich dir noch einige Gedichte:

1) Der Taucher

König, Zecher,   Knappe voll Kühnheit
wirft Becher.   springt wieder rein.
rein ins Meer.   Da lacht König Zecher
Knappe her.   die Brandung wird schwächer
Knappe munter,   futsch ist der Schwiegersohn,
spring runter.   futsch ist der Becher.
Kommt wieder aus Land,
Becher in der Hand.   * rin = rein
König sagt: (sächsische Mundart)
wer noch einmal wagt
sich rein
darf Tochter frei'n.

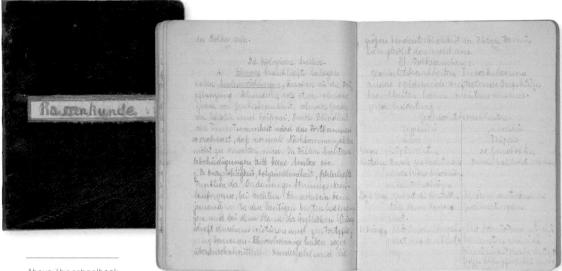

Above: This schoolbook contains notes on *Rassenkunde* (race science). It belonged to a young Jewish girl from Cologne. *Rassenkunde* became a key part of German education. Countless Jewish students had to sit through lessons about the supposed superiority of the 'Aryan' race and the inferiority of the Jews'.

Opposite top: Hitler Youth member Werner Lehmann sent this letter to his American pen pal in January 1937. Alongside descriptions of his Christmas holidays, Werner writes in broken English, 'The Jews live in our country like guests … they had take us away our independent way of thinking and had infected our race. Therefore we don't like them'.

Opposite bottom: Children's toys showing Nazi figures.

State of Terror

As the Nazis tightened their grip on Germany, their network of terror grew. The violence that had been a hallmark of their route to power was now harnessed as an instrument of government. It was unleashed on anyone who resisted the will of the regime or was considered by the Nazis to be outside the national community.

The Nazis' security network attempted to maintain complete control over Germans' everyday lives. The *Schutzstaffel* (SS) became their main enforcers of ideology. Under Himmler's leadership, this became a vast system of different parts, including the secret intelligence agencies, the *Sicherheitsdienst* (SD) and the *Gestapo*. These agencies attempted to monitor anyone suspected of rebellion – whether real or imagined. Those considered guilty were beaten, tortured and sometimes killed. Before long, the German police assisted in these activities – and the legal system helped to legitimise them.

An early decree from Hitler allowed increased state intervention into people's private lives, permitting officials to censor mail, eavesdrop on phone conversations and search private homes. Neighbours informed on neighbours, having been encouraged to believe that any perceived enemies of the Nazi state were enemies of the German people. For victims

Ein kleiner SA-Mann

of this growing persecution, there were few places to turn. The first concentration camps opened almost as soon as Hitler became chancellor. These quickly developed into feared places where people considered enemies of the state were sent in an effort to force them to comply with the will of the regime.

In the early years of the regime, most concentration camps were opened in empty buildings such as schools, disused factories and prisons. Those sent to them were mainly political opponents of the Nazis. Before long, their population was expanded to include career criminals and those the Nazis considered 'asocials'. Prisoners were held without trial for indefinite periods and with no legal protection. At first both the SA and SS ran concentration camps, but by 1934 they came under the sole command of the SS.

Dachau and Oranienburg, near Munich and Berlin respectively, were the earliest concentration camps, opening in March 1933. Dachau was established in an abandoned munitions factory outside Munich and became the 'model camp' where SS guards were trained in the use of various violent techniques to maintain control over prisoners. Hard labour was particularly favoured as a punishment technique, with Jewish prisoners being subjected to the most back-breaking work.

Left: Hitler is pictured here with a boy dressed up in an SA uniform. He was often photographed with children, whom he considered to be the soldiers of the future. In 1938 he said: 'This generation of youth is learning nothing other than to think German and act German… and they won't free themselves for the rest of their lives'.

Hitler's Political Soldiers

The SS was originally created as Hitler's private protection squad. It grew from 290 members in 1929 — when it was placed under Heinrich Himmler's authority — to over 50,000 by 1933. By 1934 it had replaced the SA in stature and importance.

SS men were passionate and committed Nazis who valued their reputation for ruthlessness. SS members had to swear a personal oath to Hitler, pledging to give their lives for him if required. Their motto 'my loyalty is my honour' was carried on the SS service dagger *(left)* and the 'death's head' insignia on their cap indicated their willingness to die for their cause. Once admitted to the SS, men were expected to devote body and soul to the organisation. They were supposed to remain physically fit and mentally committed. Alongside sports clubs, the organisation also had its own newspaper, *Das Schwarze Korps* (*The Black Corps*).

The Longest Hatred

Antisemitism has deep roots. It first emerged from a Christian hatred towards Jews and over time developed into a much wider bigotry. The Nazis exploited these long-held prejudices, embracing paranoid beliefs about a secret Jewish conspiracy for world domination.

Anti-Jewish prejudice has led to individuals and communities becoming the subject of hostility and hatred for thousands of years. This has appeared in many countries and cultures. It has fuelled grotesque stereotypes about behaviour, beliefs and physical appearance.

Left: Der Giftpilz (*The Poisonous Mushroom*) was a children's book published in 1938 by Julius Streicher, editor of the violently antisemitic paper *Der Stürmer* (*The Striker*). The book claimed Jews were like poisonous mushrooms – difficult to recognise, but potent threats to the health and survival of the *Volk*. It aimed to teach children how to identify Jews within German society.

Theodor Eicke

Theodor Eicke, an SS officer, became commandant of Dachau in the summer of 1933. The following year he was promoted to be overseer of all concentration camps. He was a committed Nazi who took great pride in developing concentration camps as places of terror and intimidation. When the SS conducted a purge of the SA in the so-called 'Night of the Long Knives', Eicke personally executed SA leader Ernst Röhm. This confirmed both the domination of the SS and Eicke's own brutal reputation.

Race Laws

In 1935 Hitler introduced new race laws at the annual Nazi Party rally in Nuremberg. These became known as the Nuremberg laws and were a significant development in antisemitic discrimination in Germany. By attempting officially to define who was Jewish, they provided a legal framework for the persecution of Jewish people. The introduction of the laws meant that anyone classified as 'a Jew' was stripped of the protection of full German citizenship and denied basic rights.

While the Nazis believed that Jewishness was a racial, not religious identity, their failure to find any scientific evidence for this forced them to use religious practice as a basis for the legal classification they used. This meant that many of those whom the laws identified as Jewish had never identified as Jewish themselves. Under the provision of the laws, a person was defined as Jewish based on how many observant Jewish grandparents they had, even if they were not personally religiously observant. Anyone now defined as 'a Jew' was prohibited from marrying or having sex with a non-Jewish German – such relationships were considered to be 'race-defilement'. Many Germans informed on those they suspected of this new crime. An industry in professional genealogy boomed across Germany as people went to increasingly great efforts to prove their non-Jewish ancestry.

Opposite top: The SA opened Oranienburg camp outside Berlin in March 1933. Rumours about what happened there swiftly made it notorious, both in Germany and abroad. Its first commandant, Werner Schäfer, wrote this book in 1934 to counter negative foreign press. He included as evidence supportive letters from British fascists who had visited the camp.

Opposite bottom: This 1935 poster published by antisemitic newspaper *Der Stürmer* calls for the death penalty for 'race defilers'.

Konzentrationslager Oranienburg

Das größte Problem!

Warum kämpft der Stürmer seit 1923 und klärt seit dieser Zeit das deutsche Volk in der Judenfrage und Rassenfrage auf? Warum sagt der Stürmer den Kampf vor allem dem

jüdischen Rassenschänder

an? Warum erließ der Führer im Jahre 1935 die Nürnberger Gesetze? Warum ließ er die Rassenschande zum

kriminellen Verbrechen

erklären und es mit Zuchthaus bestrafen?
Der Stürmer hatte von Anfang erkannt, daß der Jude gerade durch das Verbrechen der Rassenschande in der deutschen Frauen- und Mädchenwelt ein

grauenhaftes Zerstörungswerk

anrichtet. Das Zerstörungswerk der Schändung der deutschen Rasse, der Vergiftung des deutschen Blutes, der Zersetzung des deutschen Volkes.

Der Jude begeht aber trotz Nürnberger Gesetze und drakonischer Zuchthausstrafen, auch heute noch Tausende von Rassenverbrechen unter deutschen Frauen und Mädchen.

Es gibt immer noch Millionen Männer und Frauen, die von der Rassenfrage keine Ahnung haben. Sie haben sich bisher wenig oder garnicht um dieses ernste Problem gekümmert. Sie wissen nichts von der ungeheuren Wichtigkeit und von der Tragweite dieser Frage. Sie wissen nicht, daß der Führer gerade hierüber in seinem Buche „Mein Kampf" folgendes schrieb:

> Wenn man dieser einzigen Frage gegenüber alle anderen Probleme des Lebens prüft und vergleicht, dann wird man erst ersehen, wie lächerlich klein sie, hieran gemessen, sind.

Diesen Millionen Gleichgültigen, Unaufgeklärten und Unwissenden müssen die Augen geöffnet werden. Die Stürmer-Sondernummer

Todesstrafe für Rassenschänder

gibt über diese Frage gründlichste Aufklärung.

Männer und Frauen! Holt Euch Aufklärung. Sorgt dafür, daß auch andere aufgeklärt werden. Werbt neue Stürmer-Kämpfer. Gebt die Sondernummer von Hand zu Hand. Gebt Sie hinein in die Büros, in die Betriebe, in die Häuser, gebt sie in die letzte Bauernhütte. Werdet fanatische Antisemiten, werdet überzeugte Judengegner. Ihr schlagt damit die größte Schlacht für das deutsche Volk und für die nichtjüdische Menschheit.

Der Stürmer

CHAPTER THREE

Growing Isolation

A s the Nazis grew in strength and control, they used their powers of state to make life more and more difficult for Jewish people in the Reich. All levels of German government passed laws aimed at limiting opportunities open to Jews. Legislation was created at a national level that barred access to jobs and education, and state and local restrictions were developed that prevented entry to communal spaces such as parks and restaurants. While policies were handed down from the party elite, local Nazis used considerable initiative to ensure they were developed and enforced. In just a few years, this cumulative volume of legislation stripped German Jews of the rights and protections they had enjoyed for generations. Eventually more than 400 laws were introduced, each one further excluding Jews from society.

Opposite: Laws that barred Jews from day-to-day activities increased their fear and sense of isolation. Dora Francken did not feel safe developing this photograph until she had left Germany. She is standing beside notices outside a swimming pool at Blaubeuren. One reads 'No entry for Jews', the other 'Dogs not admitted'.

Right: From spring 1935, local Nazi members put up their own signs in public places in towns and villages. This street sign from Eisenach reads 'Jews are not wanted in our district'. Although the signs did not legally prevent Jews from entering places, they fuelled the cruel culture of persecution.

Für Juden keine Ordination.

As Jews were increasingly driven from public life, they were also robbed of their income and savings through targeted taxes and charges. Further regulations stripped them of the right to own businesses or property. The Nazis' intention was both to generate money for the German state and to encourage Jewish emigration. In reality, the number of people leaving fluctuated considerably. Moving abroad was difficult and the financial costs of doing so were high. These challenges were exacerbated by the inaction of foreign governments who did little to help. As time went on, Jews were increasingly unseen in everyday community life in the Reich – they were unwanted in their homeland and unwelcome anywhere else.

The Reich Expands

On 12 March 1938 German troops marched unopposed into Austria, as Hitler began to fulfil his longstanding ambition to unite the nation of his birth with Germany. The next month,

Above: This sign reading 'No prescriptions for Jews' was placed outside an 'Aryan' doctor's surgery.

Opposite: A law passed in 1938 required German Jews to apply for a new version of their *Kennkarte* (identification card). Both these newly issued *Kennkarten*, as well as passports held by Jews, were stamped with the letter 'J' for *Jude* (Jew). This development in formalised antisemitic discrimination further segregated Jews from society, making them identifiable to whoever saw the documents.

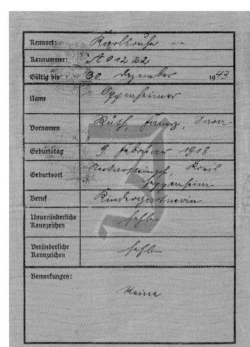

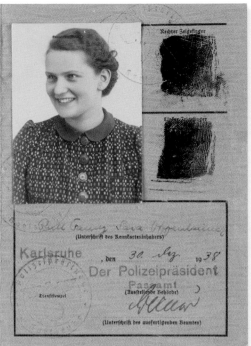

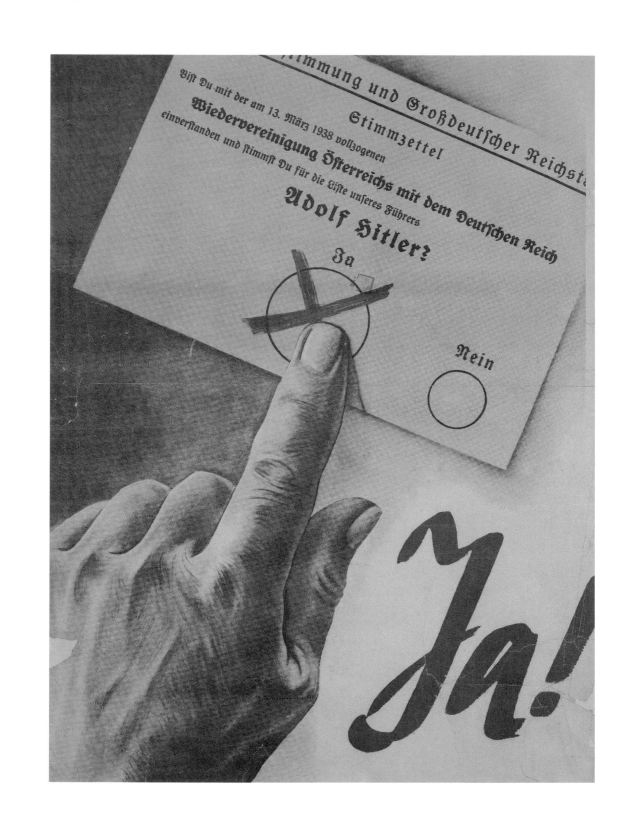

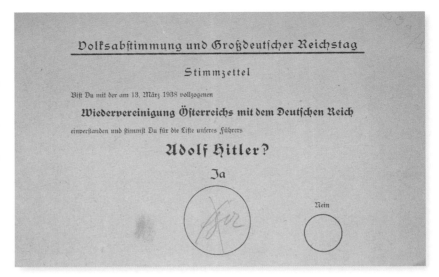

Volksabstimmung und Großdeutscher Reichstag

Stimmzettel

Bist Du mit der am 13. März 1938 vollzogenen

Wiedervereinigung Österreichs mit dem Deutschen Reich

einverstanden und stimmst Du für die Liste unseres Führers

Adolf Hitler?

Ja

Nein

a rigged referendum was forced through to confirm the *Anschluss* (union) between the countries, in contravention of the Treaty of Versailles. The *Anschluss* was widely celebrated within the expanded Reich, but had devastating consequences for more than 185,000 Austrian Jews who now found themselves living under Nazi control.

In an outbreak of antisemitic violence days after the arrival of German troops, Jews in Vienna were dragged into the streets by local antisemites – including Nazis – to be abused and humiliated in events that drew large crowds of onlookers. The ferocious and public nature of this cruelty was more extreme than anything yet seen in Germany, and took senior

Adolf Eichmann

Adolf Eichmann, a travelling salesman for an American oil company, joined the SS in 1932. He used a brief visit to Palestine in 1937 to claim expertise in Jewish affairs. By 1938 he was in charge of the Nazis' Central Office for Jewish Emigration in Vienna. Each day people crowded into his building to pay for the papers they needed to escape antisemitic persecution in Austria. His process of financial exploitation was so efficient that it was later rolled out in Germany.

Nazis in Germany by surprise. Laws were quickly passed with the aim of excluding Austrian Jews from public life, businesses were boycotted, closed or 'Aryanised' and Jewish employees were dismissed.

Under the combined threat of targeted violence in the streets and increasing restrictions on their rights to live and work, pressure mounted on Jews in Austria to leave their home country. Within a year, nearly half of them had left.

Six months after the *Anschluss*, Hitler demanded control over the German-speaking areas of Czechoslovakia, known as the Sudetenland. This created a crisis that brought Europe to the brink of war. Hoping to avoid another devastating European conflict, the British, French and Italian leaders met with Hitler in Munich and agreed to allow Germany to annex this territory. In open violation of the agreement, German forces seized the remaining Czech provinces of Bohemia and Moravia in March 1939. Jews in these areas faced an uncertain future.

We, the German Führer and Chancellor and the
British Prime Minister, have had a further
meeting today and are agreed in recognising that
the question of Anglo-German relations is of the
first importance for the two countries and for
Europe.

We regard the agreement signed last night
and the Anglo-German Naval Agreement as symbolic
of the desire of our two peoples never to go to
war with one another again.

We are resolved that the method of
consultation shall be the method adopted to deal
with any other questions that may concern our two
countries, and we are determined to continue our
efforts to remove possible sources of difference
and thus to contribute to assure the peace of
Europe.

Neville Chamberlain

September 30. 1938.

A Violent Escalation

On 9 November 1938, the first state-sponsored campaign of mass violence against Jews erupted across Germany and Austria. Rampaging Nazi mobs attacked both Jewish people and Jewish-owned property in public spaces and private homes in cities, towns and villages across the Reich. Nearly half the synagogues in Germany were burned down and tens of thousands of men were sent to concentration camps.

The onslaught was presented as a spontaneous act of revenge by the German people for the murder of a Nazi diplomat in France by the Jewish teenager Herschel Grynszpan. In reality, it was instigated, orchestrated and approved by senior Nazis. Grynszpan – who had been born in Germany but was living in Paris – had become enraged when he learned his family had been evicted from Germany to their native Poland because they were Jewish. Seeking revenge, he travelled to the German embassy and shot diplomat Ernst vom Rath in the abdomen. Vom Rath's death two days later coincided with events traditionally held by the Nazis on 9 November in recognition of the failed putsch in 1923. Senior members of the inner circle, who were all together at a function in Munich, seized on the news to demand violent revenge against all Jews in the Reich. With Hitler's approval, propaganda minister Joseph Goebbels gave the orders that initiated the violence. Further orders from Reinhard Heydrich established how these 'spontaneous' actions should happen. Instructions were sent to local Nazi leaders in a co-ordinated way, but in practice the attacks were both chaotic and lawless.

Fuelled by alcohol, local SA units led mobs who roamed the streets. They were joined by SS members, local schoolchildren and Hitler Youth. Many of the SA and SS were dressed in civilian clothes in order to give the impression that the violence was being carried out by the public at large. Although their target was both property and people, they were under explicit instructions to avoid damaging buildings belonging to non-Jewish citizens. Any Jews they found were humiliated, terrorised and victimised both in the streets and in their own homes. Some women were sexually assaulted. All conspicuous signs of Jewish culture and religious observance were targeted, and

Opposite top: Religious items were deliberately targeted by the mobs during the violence. This *tallit* (prayer shawl) was found among debris in Vienna on the morning after. Germany's only remaining Jewish newspaper published requests seeking replacement items. This allowed religious services to continue – but only where the Nazis permitted.

Opposite bottom: This synagogue in Berlin was destroyed during the anti-Jewish attacks on 9 and 10 November 1938.

Left: The Nazis blamed Jews themselves for the violence and fined them one billion Reichsmarks to pay for damage done to their own property. A punishing 20 per cent tax was imposed on all of their reported assets to cover this sum. Jews in Bremen – and across the Reich – were also forced to clean up the wreckage.

Opposite: Jewish men sent to concentration camps after the pogrom were allowed to send postcards to family or friends, which helped create an illusion that their imprisonment was legal. This postcard was sent from Dachau by Otto Patriasz to his wife, Margarethe. The postcards were often the first news families received about their loved ones' whereabouts – sometimes weeks after they had been detained – and the content was heavily censored.

before destroying synagogues mobs were ordered to seize all of the records in them. These records were transferred to the Nazi intelligence agency, the *Sicherheitsdienst* (SD), and were used to help trace and arrest local Jewish people.

Approximately 7,500 Jewish-owned businesses were destroyed and stock was often stolen, despite official orders forbidding it. Nazi minister Hermann Göring was furious about the overall cost of the damage, fearing that insurance pay-outs and the lost opportunities to 'Aryanise' these businesses would affect a German economy that was already short of money. During the attacks more than 90 people were killed. None of their murderers were ever punished.

The Nazis described the events as *Kristallnacht* ('The Night of Broken Glass'), a name that has traditionally been used to describe the attacks in the years since. However, this term cloaks the reality of the violence, referring by inference only to attacks against property, not people. It was instantly described elsewhere at the time as a 'pogrom' – a Russian word from the 1800s referring to large-scale assaults on Jews. The violence caused international outrage. Some Germans also opposed it, but few spoke out. For the first time, many Jews now felt their lives were in danger.

18. XI · 38

Mein liebes Greterl! Teile Dir mit, dass ich gesund und munter bin, hoffe dasselbe von Dir. Meine Adresse lautet: O. Patriasz Dachau 3K geb. 24. XII. 1898 Block 24, Stube 1. Bei Postanweisungen muss diese Adresse auch auf der Rückseite des kleinen Abschnittes (Absenderadresse) vermerkt werden. Geld kann ich jede Woche empfangen. Alle Post muss mit Tinte geschrieben werden. Nur ungefütterte Konverts verwenden.

Kuss Otto

The pogrom sent shockwaves across the world and made international headlines for weeks. American and British newspapers expressed horror at the dramatic turn of events in a 'civilised' nation. Many publications compared it with the barbaric pogroms of the Middle Ages. Although many people actively participated, a large number of Germans were ashamed by the level of violence and destruction. One newspaper reported that over one hundred 'Aryan Germans' were arrested by police in Berlin for disapproving of the attacks. Partially as a response to these reactions, the Nazis decided that, instead of stopping the violence, they would move it off the streets and away from public scrutiny.

Senseless Fury

In the days after the pogrom, over 26,000 Jewish men were interned in Buchenwald, Dachau and Sachsenhausen concentration camps. For the first time, Jewish prisoners made up the majority of the camps' population – if only briefly. Many of the new prisoners were taken directly from streets, trams and cafés – as well as from their own homes. The camps were unprepared for this huge influx of people and became vastly overcrowded. To secure release, the incarcerated men needed to prove their intention to emigrate. Their families tried

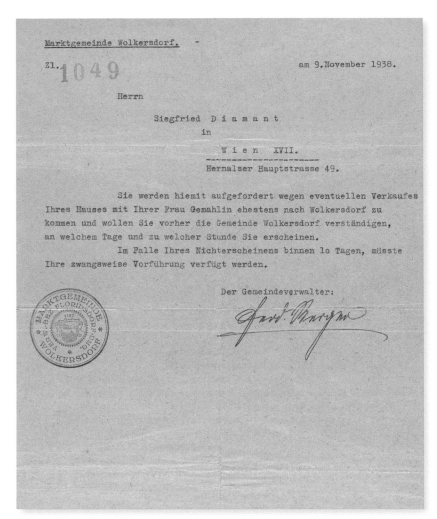

Marktgemeinde Wolkersdorf. -

Zl. 1049   am 9.November 1938.

                Herrn

                Siegfried D i a m a n t
                        in

                        W i e n XVII.
                        Hernalser Hauptstrasse 49.

        Sie werden hiemit aufgefordert wegen eventuellen Verkaufes
Ihres Hauses mit Ihrer Frau Gemahlin ehestens nach Wolkersdorf zu
kommen und wollen Sie vorher die Gemeinde Wolkersdorf verständigen,
an welchem Tage und zu welcher Stunde Sie erscheinen.
        Im Falle Ihres Nichterscheinens binnen lo Tagen, müsste
Ihre zwangsweise Vorführung verfügt werden.

                        Der Gemeindeverwalter:

Left and opposite: Siegfried and Irma Diamant began preparations to leave Austria in October 1938. Seven months later they arrived in Britain with their young daughter Charlotte. The convoluted emigration process that the family had to undergo to secure a visa involved hundreds of pieces of paper.

These are a few examples of the many documents the Diamant family had to assemble in order to emigrate. Like all families wanting to find refuge in Britain, as well as proving their identity and financial standing they also had to submit formal proof of their mental and physical wellbeing.

Left: Letter for forced sale of the Diamant home.

Opposite clockwise from top left: Certificate of good conduct; proof of birth; certificate from finance office.

frantically to obtain the necessary paperwork. Due to terrible over-crowding, poor sanitation and abuse by the SS, hundreds of Jewish prisoners had died by the end of the year.

Nowhere to Belong

As Jewish people living within the Reich came under increasing assault during the 1930s, more and more of them looked to emigrate. The numbers of prospective emigrants had developed inconsistently in the preceeding years, but swelled quickly following the terrifying violence which accompanied the

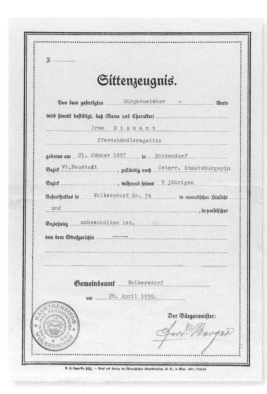

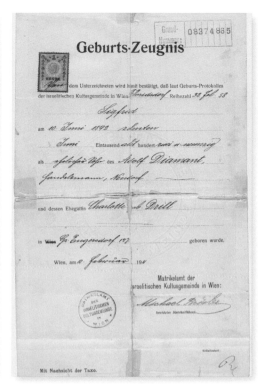

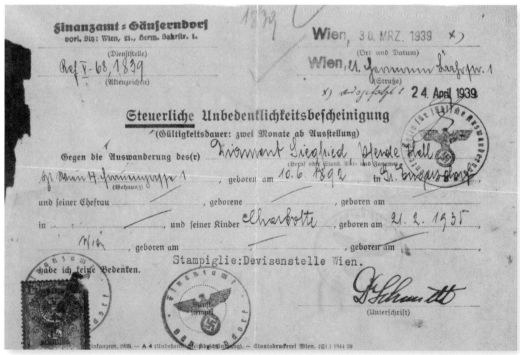

Dr. Alfred Schwarz
    Wien VI.,
Gumpendorferstr.72

M E D I C A L   C E R T I F I C A T E

Place: VIENNA

Date: .... 4/3 ...1939.

I hereby certify that I have examined

Mr. *Adolf Blond* ....

and find .*him*., not to be mentally or physically defective in any

way, that ..*he*.. is not afflicted with tuberculosis in any form

or with an infectious, loathsome or contagious disease, that

....*he*. is not suffering from favus, leprosy, framboesia or yaws,

trachoma, syphilis or scabies.

.....*J. V. S. Groag*...........

Medical adviser to the
British Consulate.

Mentally defective includes:

Idiots
Imbeciles
Feebleminded persons
Insane persons
Epileptics
Persons having previously had attacks of insanity
Persons of constitutional psychopathic inferiority
Persons suffering from chronic alcoholism.

I also certify that *Mr. Adolf Blond* ....

has never been in a mental hospital nor in prison.

Vienna,........ 4/3 ...1939.   *J. V. S. Groag.*

C o p y .

17th July, 1939.

Ref.No. BA/22870.

Dr. Alfons Lasker
Kaiser Wilhelmstrasse 69,
Breslau 13.
Germany.

Dear Sir,

Further to our letter of the 22nd June, and
yours of the 11th July enquiring as to
the position of your case, we regret to
inform you that we are unable to proceed
with the matter in view of your very high
waiting number for America.

In view of this decision we advise you to
endeavour to obtain alternative plans
for re-emigration and, on receipt of
such information, we assure you that
we will do our utmost to assist you.

Yours faithfully
German Jewish Aid Committee
signed G.J.Horsfall

Immigration Department.

Anschluss and the 1938 pogrom. Tens of thousands of Jews tried desperately to escape, convinced they were no longer safe in the places their families had called home for generations. Their frantic search for asylum in countries across the world sparked an international refugee crisis. Only a fraction of those who tried to leave succeeded.

The growing problems faced by Jews in the Reich during the 1930s were widely known by governments across the world, but

Sending Children Away

In Britain, public reaction to the November pogrom sparked a parliamentary debate on refugees. The British government agreed to allow entry for Jewish and 'non-Aryan' children, on the condition that they would not be a burden on the state. The first child refugees arrived in Britain on 2 December 1938. This group included more than 200 children from a Jewish orphanage in Berlin that had been destroyed in the November pogrom. Thousands more would follow, leaving Germany on what became known as the *Kindertransport* (children's transport).

The *Kindertransport* were not co-ordinated by the state, but by individuals and organisations within the Reich and refugee aid committees in Britain. Some priority was given to children who were orphaned or homeless and to those whose parents were in concentration camps or no longer able to support them financially. Each child needed a sponsor to give a guarantee declaring they had enough funding for the child's care, education and eventual return. The children were offered temporary refuge, not permanent asylum. Most people in Britain thought the crisis would pass and that the children would go back to their parents. Parents across the Reich were forced to make the agonising choice to separate from their children, entrusting them to the care of strangers.

The experiences of children who arrived on the *Kindertransport* varied considerably. Some found support and affection from their carers, while others faced maltreatment and neglect. Separated from their families and in unfamiliar surroundings, many were lonely and desperately unhappy.

Left: Musician, journalist and scientist Walter Finkler often travelled for work and would bring back gifts for his daughter Evelyn. He hid them in coat pockets for her to find. This toy dog was his parting gift to her before she left Vienna on a *Kindertransport* at the age of eight.

Opposite left: Each child needed a sponsor to give a guarantee declaring they had enough funding for the child's care, education and eventual return.

Right: In a letter to her parents, Ruth Neumeyer described how she and her friend Jane often played the recorder together. Her father Hans, a composer, sent his daughter sheet music of duets he had written for the girls. On the cover was a drawing that suggests how Ruth's parents imagined her life in England.

Below right: Karoline Koniec, who was living in Bratislava, hoped to be able to join her children Dori and Herbi – who had left on the *Kindertransport* – in Britain. She asked Dori to write to her in English so she could practise her language skills. Younger children, like Karoline's son Herbl, often lost their first language as they adjusted to their new surroundings, making communication with their parents more difficult. In a separate letter, he wrote in English 'I hope you will be able to understand me as I cannot speak your language any more'.

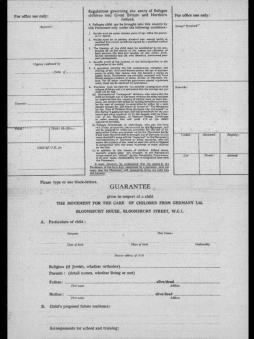

Shelter Through Domestic Service

Alongside the *Kindertransport*, thousands of Jewish women from the Reich were allowed to come to Britain as refugee domestic servants – predominantly cooks, maids or housekeepers. They were only permitted entry if they had guaranteed employment. The government's decision to admit these migrants was driven largely by a shortage of British servants for middle-class households. It was difficult work, with long hours and low pay. Many of those applying worked in completely different jobs, but were desperate to leave the Reich however they could. Around 50,000 women eventually came to work in domestic service. Some were barely older than the children on the *Kindertransport*.

Left: Hortense Heidenfeld had ambitions to be a doctor, but came to Britain as a domestic servant at the age of 18. She worked for the Hunts, a family similar to her own. In this letter, her father describes how he and his wife shared the Hunts' interests, like hunting and dog breeding. He thanks them for allowing Hortense to enjoy their home, which resembled the one they used to own, and for their kind treatment of his daughter.

little assistance was offered. While it may have been the Nazis' intention to compel Jewish people to leave, they had made them 'undesirable aliens' for foreign governments by taking their money and possessions. Most countries retained strict quotas for the number of refugees they would accept, forcing emigrants to prove they could live without state support before offering them visas. In July 1938, representatives from 32 countries met at Évian-les-Bains in France to discuss the growing refugee crisis. While most countries expressed sympathy for Jews in the Reich, only the Dominican Republic offered to accept additional asylum seekers.

Hopeful emigrants had to overcome enormous obstacles. Visa applications were costly and complicated. Securing the necessary paperwork could take months. Even the few successful applicants could face waiting lists of up to 11 years. Distrust of foreigners in an era of economic crisis meant that no one wanted to accept large numbers of immigrants. For the men, women and children fleeing, the destination was less important than finding somewhere, anywhere, to go. As the threat of a major European war grew, opportunities to escape were further reduced.

Those Who Remain

Although thousands of Jews fled the Reich during the 1930s, escape was not an option for many. Some could not afford to emigrate; some could not find anywhere to go. For others, the idea of leaving their homes was more than they could bear. The elderly, the infirm and those looking after them – mostly women – had no choice but to stay. The number of suicides increased. In the grip of an increasingly hostile regime, those left were forced to await what was to come.

CHAPTER FOUR

War

On 1 September 1939, Germany invaded Poland. Two days later Britain and France declared war on Germany. Hitler saw Poland as a land to be colonised, ordering his forces not only to conquer their enemies, but to destroy them. Germany's swift military victory was followed by a brutal occupation. Murder, forced labour and deportation were all methods the Germans used to rule their new territory and to 'purify' it of people they deemed racially inferior. The population now under Nazi control included 2.1 million Jews.

Shortly after Germany invaded Poland from the west, the Soviet Union invaded from the east. Territory was divided between the two countries as part of a secret pact and Poland disappeared from the map. The Nazis absorbed some areas directly into the Reich. Most of the remainder were designated the *Generalgouvernement* (General Government).

Six months after victory in Poland, Hitler's armies attacked western Europe, conquering every country in their path in a matter of weeks. By June 1940, they occupied Denmark, Norway, Luxembourg, the Netherlands, Belgium, France and the British Channel Islands – each of which had surrendered in quick succession. With most of Europe now under control, Hitler made plans to attack the Soviet Union. His ambition was to dominate its people, destroy its culture and political system, and claim its territory as his own. On 18 December 1940, he issued an order to prepare for invasion.

Savage Domination

Germany ruled Poland through terror. The aim of the Nazis' occupation policy was ruthlessly to exploit the country, using its land to provide both living space and material resources for Germany and its non-Jewish population as a source of slave labour. Polish language and culture would be eliminated. To remove any potential resistance, newly formed mobile execution units – known as *Einsatzgruppen* – rounded up Poland's political, religious and intellectual leadership. In a campaign entitled Operation 'Tannenberg' these units killed thousands of civilians. More than 20,000 people thought to be resisting – or capable of resisting – German occupation were murdered within weeks. By the end of the year, the number of people killed had risen to 60,000.

Mass Expulsion

The Nazis wanted to remove all Jews from any land they considered their own, a strategy they described as a 'territorial solution to the Jewish question'. At first, they proposed

Opposite: German forces capture and burn the Polish village of Goworowo, 9 September 1939.

Right: Hermann Gutmann was one of 2,500 young men designated as an 'enemy alien' and sent by the British government for internment in Australia on the HMT *Dunera.* The ship was overcrowded and conditions were terrible. On arrival, Gutmann was detained in Camp Hay. He kept a diary while there between June 1940 and October 1941.

creating a Jewish reservation under German control in eastern Poland. This was known as the Nisko plan. As part of this ill-fated scheme (overseen by Adolf Eichmann), thousands of Jews were sent to marshy, inhospitable land near Lublin in October 1939. When the logistics and practicalities of this proved too

difficult, the Nazis came up with a more fantastical plan –
the mass deportation of Jews to Madagascar, an island off the
coast of East Africa. Although leading Nazis believed millions
of Jews could be deported to the island, they did not care how
they would survive once there. The idea, however, depended
on imminent victory in the war in order to gain access to the
necessary sea routes and was eventually abandoned. Ultimately
attempts to implement a 'territorial solution' were unsuccessful
and the Nazis looked to other 'solutions'.

From Exiles to 'Enemies'

At the outbreak of war, around 70,000 Austrians and Germans
in the UK were immediately classified as 'enemy aliens' by
the British government. Most were Jewish refugees who had
fled Nazi persecution and now found themselves identified as
possible threats to Britain's security. In the summer of 1940,
when a German invasion seemed imminent, up to 27,000 of
these 'enemy aliens' were interned in specially created camps.
Some of the camps were in the United Kingdom, others much
further away in Canada and Australia.

In 1939, the Council for German Jewry opened a refugee
camp in Kent for Jewish male immigrants from the Reich.
Known as the Kitchener Camp, it housed men who had been
released from concentration camps on condition that they left
Germany immediately. When war broke out, many of these
refugees wanted to help fight the Nazis and attempted to join the
British Army – something which they were eventually able to do.

Outcast

As German forces advanced through eastern Europe, they
established ghettos. These were specially designated areas
within towns, cities and villages in Nazi-occupied territory
where Jews were forced to live. In total, at least 1,100 ghettos
were set up by the Germans during the Second World War.
They varied substantially in terms of size, composition and
length of existence. The largest, in Warsaw, had over 400,000
inhabitants, while smaller ghettos in rural locations had a few
hundred. They were used by the Nazis as a means of both

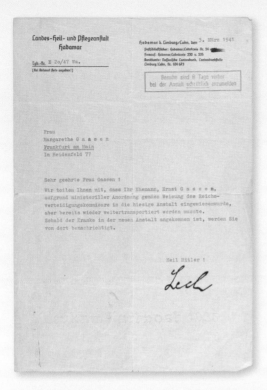

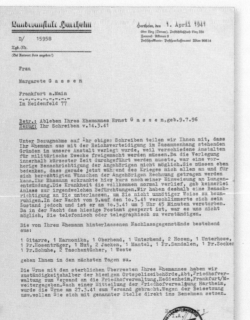

Medicine and Mass Murder

Shortly after the outbreak of war, Hitler signed an order authorising the murder of disabled people in the Reich. Described as a 'euthanasia programme', this was an inaugural policy of state-sanctioned mass murder that initially targeted children before being expanded to include adults. The programme was a radicalisation of earlier Nazi policies relating to disability – and what the Nazis considered to be 'hereditary defects'. It was instigated by a request from the father of a disabled baby to Hitler asking for permission to have his son killed.

Hitler entrusted the order authorising the 'euthanasia programme' to Philipp Bouhler and Karl Brandt, giving both men responsibility for co-ordinating the large system put in place to arrange the murders. They were helped by selected medical professionals. The euthanasia order was the only time Hitler personally signed documents linking him to mass murder. Doctors working in the programme decided who to kill by verifying forms submitted by other medics. If they were in agreement that the 'patient' should be 'euthanised' it was recorded on the document, and the individual was sent to a euthanasia 'clinic'. Parents were not consulted and were usually lied to about how their children had died. The programme was supposed to be secret. It was suspended after knowledge of it led to public protests within Germany. By then tens of thousands had been murdered.

Left: Dr Ernst Gassen was a married father of two who worked as a doctor near Leipzig. In 1937 he was struck off for opposing the Nazis. He became extremely depressed and was eventually sent to an asylum. From there he was transferred to the Hartheim euthanasia facility where he was murdered. The Hartheim euthanasia clinic sent these letters to his wife Margarete, falsely claiming that he died of pneumonia.

segregation and control and were formed at different times and in different ways. While some existed for only a few days or weeks, others lasted for many years. The majority were in the Nazi-controlled area of occupied Poland known as the *Generalgouvernment* (General Government). In some places they were situated in a city's historic 'Jewish quarter'; in others – particularly in larger cities – they were deliberately established in the poorest districts.

The development of ghettos was not determined by any single Nazi policy. Reinhard Heydrich, chief of the German Security Police, issued a *Schnellbrief* document on 21 September 1939 which laid out his instructions for *Einsatzgruppen* leaders in occupied Poland. He ordered that preparation should be made for the concentration of Jews from the countryside into designated parts of cities, but gave no indication about the nature of long-term plans. Decisions about how individual sites should be developed and run were largely left to local Nazi officials. These administrators controlled who – and what – could enter or leave. They also controlled economies within ghettos and managed the exploitation of ghetto residents for cheap labour. The location of individual ghettos and the decisions of the Nazis as to who ran them had a profound impact on the people confined within them.

The creation of ghettos was part of a larger Nazi strategy to reshape the territory and people of eastern Europe in the image of the Reich. Centralising Jews within their boundaries separated them from the rest of the population as part of the broader plan to remove them entirely – though at this stage there was no overall policy about how this objective should be achieved. Non-Jewish Polish people were moved into spaces 'left vacant' by Jews forced into ghettos and 'ethnic Germans' were given properties vacated by Poles. Nazi plans for post-war Europe imagined that non-Jewish populations who could not be 'germanised' would be denied any form of education and would be enslaved. Under these plans, tens of millions would be allowed to die through starvation or forced relocation in what was considered by the Nazis to be natural wastage.

At first most ghettos remained unenclosed, or 'open', meaning that although restrictions were placed on where Jews could live or go, some degree of movement was still permitted.

Opposite: At first ghettos were used to centralise Jews from nearby areas. Over time they were increasingly populated with people deported from other countries. This brought together individuals from a wide range of backgrounds who spoke many different languages. Translation services – as advertised in this sign – were in high demand.

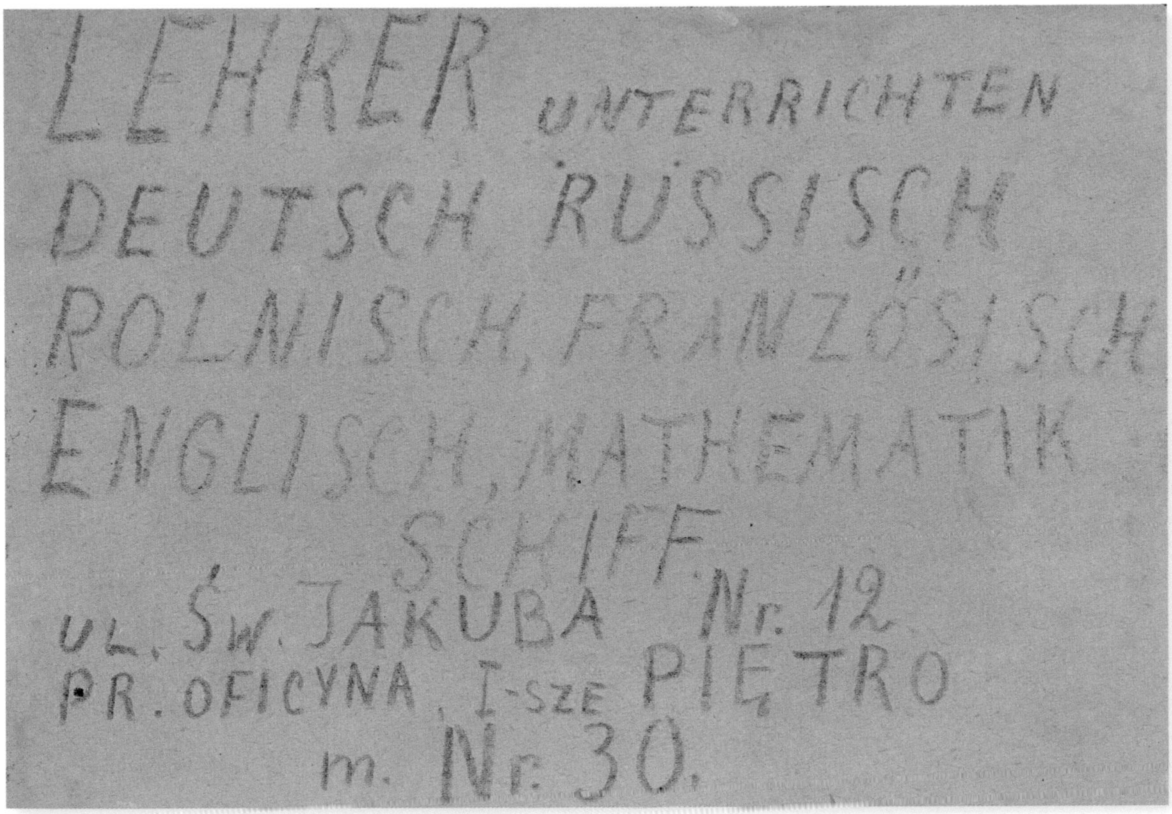

LEHRER UNTERRICHTEN
DEUTSCH RUSSISCH
POLNISCH, FRANZÖSISCH
ENGLISCH, MATHEMATIK
SCHIFF.
UL. ŚW. JAKUBA Nr. 12.
PR. OFICYNA, I-SZE PIĘTRO
m. Nr. 30.

From 1940 the Nazis began to enclose ghettos with walls and fences in order to seal them from the outside world and prevent unpermitted entry or exit. This sealing of ghettos restricted the transit of goods which led to a rapid deterioration in conditions. In the larger ghettos Jews organised self-aid and social welfare to help the most vulnerable residents, but despite these efforts death rates climbed steeply.

Between the Germans and the *Judenrat*

In order to try and ensure the smooth running of ghettos, the Germans created *Judenräte* (Jewish councils) as intermediaries between the Nazi occupation authorities and Jewish communities. These were designed to manage day-to-day administration and oversee the efficient implementation of Nazi orders. *Judenrat* members were usually men who had been

DER STADTKOMMISSAR
Abtlg. I a.

Neu-Sandez, den 12. November 1941.

ANORDNUNG NR. 59.

An die jüdische Bevölkerung der Stadt Neu-Sandez!

Zur Klarstellung des bestehenden Rechtszustandes wird hiermit bekanntgegeben:

1.) Den in der Stadt Neu-Sandez wohnhaften Juden ist das in meiner Anordnung Nr. 51 vom 14. 6. 1941 festgesetzte Gebiet als „Jüdisches Wohngebiet" zugewiesen.

2.) Die Juden haben zwischen dem jüdischen Wohnbezirk jenseits der Kamienica und dem jüdischen Wohnbezirk in der Altstadt einen freien Verbindungsweg über Wall-, Schweden-, und Pijarenstrasse. Es besteht ferner ein freier Zugang zum Rathaus **nur** über die Piastenstrasse.

3.) Nach § 4 - b der III. Verordnung über Aufenthaltsbeschränkungen im Generalgouvernement vom 15. 10. 1941 werden Juden, die den ihnen zugewiesenen Wohnbezirk unbefugt verlassen, mit dem Tode bestraft. Die gleiche Strafe trifft Personen, die solchen Juden Unterschlupf gewähren. Anstifter und Gehilfen werden wie die Täter, die versuchte Tat wird wie die vollendete mit dem Tode bestraft. In leichteren Fällen kann auf Zuchthaus oder Gefängnis erkannt werden. Die Aburteilung erfolgt durch die Sondergerichte.

In Ausnahmefällen werden von mir zum Betreten des arischen Wohngebietes in der Stadt Neu-Sandez gelbe Passierscheine erteilt.

Inhaber des gelben Passierscheins dürfen im übrigen die Haupt- und Krakauerstrasse sowie den Ringplatz nur dann betreten, wenn das Ziel **nicht** auf anderem Wege erreichbar ist.

4.) Das Verlassen der Stadt Neu-Sandez kann nur in besonders begründeten Ausnahmefällen gestattet werden. In solchen Fällen werden von mir grüne Passierscheine erteilt.

5.) Die Sperrzeit für die jüdische Bevölkerung ist für die Zeit vom 1.4. bis 30. 9. von 20.30 Uhr bis 6 Uhr früh und für die Zeit vom 1. 10. bis 31. 3. von 19.30 bis 6 Uhr früh festgesetzt. In Ausnahmefällen kann die Sperrzeit verlängert werden. Hierfür erteile ich weisse Passierscheine.

6.) An Sonn- und staatlich anerkannten Feiertagen dürfen Juden den Ringplatz und die Hauptstrasse (abgesehen von dem freien Verbindungsweg zwischen den Gettoteilen) überhaupt nicht betreten. Das Herumstehen ist den Juden selbst mit gelbem Passierschein ausserhalb des jüdischen Wohnbezirkes verboten.

7.) Das jüdische Bad an der Krakauerstrasse kann **nur** von der Tarnowerstrasse über die Lelevelstrasse erreicht und wieder verlassen werden.

8.) Jüdische Leichenbegängnisse aus der Altstadt dürfen nach vorheriger Anmeldung bei der städt. Abt. für Friedhofsangelegenheiten (Ic) des Tor Krakauerstrasse 13 ausnahmsweise benutzen.

9.) Jüdische Märkte sind nur auf dem Judenmarkt und dem Höllenplatz zugelassen.

10.) Die mit Anordnung Nr. 57 verfügte Sperrung wegen Seuchengefahr wird aufgehoben.

11.) Alle bisherigen Passierscheine verlieren ab sofort ihre Gültigkeit. Sie können unter Anrechnung der Gebühren, falls die Notwendigkeit weiter besteht, bei mir (Abtlg. Ia) umgetauscht werden.

DER STADTKOMMISSAR
Dr. SCHMIDT.

Buch- und Kunstdruckerei R. Wohlwender
Neu-Sandez, Hauptstrasse 19, Fernruf Nr. 121.

DER STADTKOMMISSAR
Abtlg. I a.

Neu-Sandez, dnia 12. listopada 1941.

Zarządzenie Nr. 59.

Do żydowskiej ludności miasta Neu-Sandez!

Celem wyjaśnienia istniejącego stanu prawnego donosi się niniejszem:

1.) Mieszkającym w Neu-Sandez żydom wyznaczono, zgodnie z moim zarządzeniem Nr. 51 z 14 czerwca 1941, ustalono obszar jako „żydowska dzielnica".

2.) Żydzi mają między żydowską dzielnicą po drugiej stronie Kamienicy a żydowską dzielnicą w Starym Mieście wolną drogę łączącą przez ulicę Wałową, Szwedzką i Pijarów. Ponadto wolny dostęp do Ratusza istnieje **tylko** przez ulicę Piastów.

3.) Wedle § 4-b III. Rozporządzenia o ograniczeniach pobytu w Generalnym Gubernatorstwie z 15. 10. 1941 poniosą ci żydzi, którzy nieuprawnieni opuszczą wyznaczoną im dzielnicę, karę śmierci. Tę samą karę poniosą te osoby, które takim żydom udziela przytułku. Podżegacze i pomocnicy poniosą na równi ze sprawcami karę śmierci, usiłowany czyn, na równi z dokonanym karany będzie śmiercią. W lżejszych wypadkach można wyznaczyć karę ciężkiego więzienia albo aresztu. Zasądzenie nastąpi przez specjalnie wyznaczone sądy. W wyjątkowych wypadkach udzielane będą przezemnie dla pobytu chwilowego w aryjskich dzielnicach miasta Neu-Sandez żółte przepustki. Posiadacze żółtej przepustki mogą zresztą ulicę Główną i Krakowską jakoteż Rynek tylko w tym wypadku przekroczyć, jeśli celu **nie** mogli na innej drodze osiągnąć.

4.) Miasto Neu-Sandez będzie można opuścić tylko w wyjątkowo uzasadnionych wypadkach. W takich wypadkach udzielane będą przezemnie zielone przepustki.

5.) Dla żydowskiej ludności ruch uliczny będzie zamknięty w czasie od 1 kwietnia do 30 września między 20.30 a 6 rano a w czasie od 1 października do 31 marca między 19.30 a 6 rano. W wyjątkowych wypadkach może ten czas zamknięcia być przedłużony. Do tego udzielę białych przepustek.

6.) W niedzielę i święta przez Państwo uznane nie wolno żydom zjawiać się na Rynku i ulicy Głównej (nie wliczając jednak wolnego odcinka drogi łączącej dwie dzielnice żydowskie). Zatrzymywanie się żydów poza dzielnicami żydowskimi nawet wówczas jest zakazane, jeśli posiadają żółtą przepustkę.

7.) Łaźnia żydowska przy ulicy Krakowskiej może być dostępna i opuszczana **tylko** ulicą Lelewela.

8.) Pogrzeby żydowskie ze Starego Miasta mogą po poprzednim zgłoszeniu w oddz. miejskim dla spraw cmentarnych (I c) przechodzić wyjątkowo przez bramę ulicy Krakowskiej Nr. 13.

9.) Żydowskie targi dopuszczane są tylko na Targu żydowskim i na „Piekle".

10.) Zamknięcie, zarządzeniem Nr. 57 ustanowione z powodu epidemii, zostaje odwolane.

11.) Wszystkie dawniejsze przepustki od dnia dzisiejszego tracą swoją ważność. Mogą one być za zaliczeniem należytości, jeśli istnieje dalsza potrzeba tych przepust-k, u mnie (O. Ia) wymieniane.

DER STADTKOMMISSAR
Dr. SCHMIDT.

---

prominent representatives within pre-war Jewish society. They were forced to carry out censuses of Jews in their areas, organise labour and enforce restrictive new laws. They had personal responsibility to implement Nazis' decisions, but were able to do very little to influence what these decisions should be.

Jewish people who had to co-operate with the Germans – such as *Judenrat* members – were confronted with very specific moral and ethical dilemmas. While they were responsible for implementing Nazi policies, many also believed this enabled them to soften the impact of those policies. It also put them in a position where they could help to protect their own families. These areas of enforced collaboration have been described as the 'grey zone'. Some of those who occupied these roles became the subject of vehement criticism from other Jewish people.

Opposite: This proclamation, dated 12 November 1941, gives notice of the establishment of a 'Jewish district' in Nowy Sącz in occupied Poland. It outlined the areas where Jews were allowed to move around and warned that anyone caught outside these areas without special permission would be executed. It also threatened the death penalty for anyone caught helping or hiding Jews.

Right: Gazeta Żydowska was a Nazi-authorised newspaper for Jews in occupied-Poland. It was used as a channel to communicate information about anti-Jewish restrictions and regulations. This copy from 24 December 1940 includes information about the sealing of the Warsaw ghetto and the 'Aryanisation' of Jewish-owned businesses outside the sealed area.

Rok I Nr 45   Cena 30 gr = 15 Rpf

GAZETA ŻYDOWSKA

יודישע צייטונג

Kraków, wtorek 24 grudnia 1940

KOMUNIKATY WOJENNE

Komunikaty niemieckie
Komunikaty włoskie

Dzisiejsza „Gazeta Żydowska" zawiera:

Ważne wiadomości z Warszawy

Informacje dla rodzin wysiedlonych z Krakowa

Wiadomości z Palestyny

Jak rozpocząć prowadzenie przemysłu?

Poradnik dla gospodyń

i t. p.

Fakt Trzech Mocarstw

Gen. Antonescu obejmuje również i tekę ministra Spraw Zagranicznych

Mrozy hamują operacje w Albanii

Neutralność Jugosławii

Znaczenie naftociągu dla Anglii

Jakie siły koncentrowała Anglia nad Morzem Śródziemnym?

Nowy prezydent Finlandii wybrany

Mrozy na Syberii

Zwołanie kongresu partyjnego w Moskwie

850 tysięcy straconych dni roboczych

Szwajcaria domaga się odszkodowania

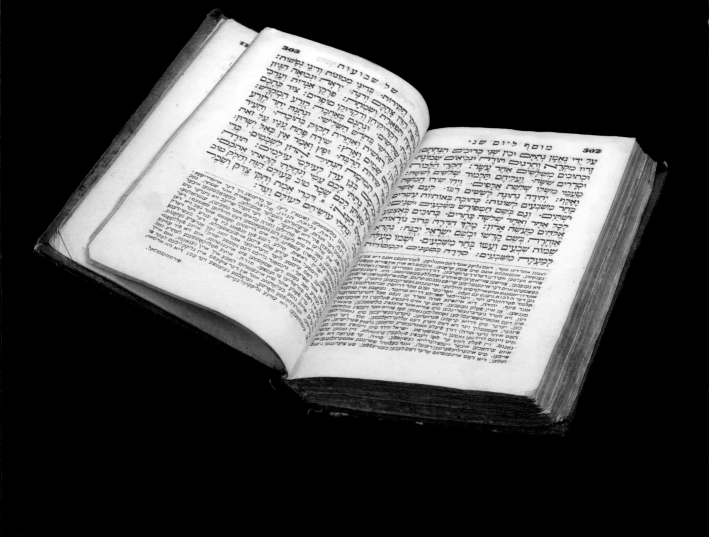

וְהַדְיָנִים שֶׁמַּדְלִיקִין וְהַדָּם הַשְּׁלִישִׁי בָּרִאשֵׁי
וּפֵרְקֵי: צִיר דִּקְקֹדֶשׁ: וְהִרְפֵּא: סוֹפְרִים יִזְרַע יָחֵד לָעֵד
וְהַדְקֹדֶשׁ שְׂדֵה פָּתַח אֵין לְשַׁבְּמִים תִּרְדְּה
בְּדִבְּרֵי יִשְׁרָאֵל עַל יִשְׂרָאֵל וְיָפֵץ וְאָמַר אֵין לְשַׁבְּמִים טוֹב
הַנְּחִיל עוֹד לָחָלֵל לַדְאָרֶץ הַזֶּה חֵלֶק טוֹב
דִּבְרֵי לְעֹלָם אָמַר וָעֵד: עֵדֶן עַם טוֹב בְּעֵלָם צֶדֶק וְשֵׂכֶל

עַל יְדֵי נָאֱמְן נֶחְתַּם וְכֵן שָׁנֵי כְרוּבִים הַפְּתָחִים
וְכָתוּב מִשְׁלֹשִׁים וְחֵרוּגִים תַּרְדָּה וְיִקְרָאִים שְׁמוֹנָה
וּכְתוּבִים שִׁשָּׁה: וְעֲלֵיהֶם הַקָּרֵא שְׁלֹשָׁה הַשִּׁשָּׁה
וִיקָרִים מִשְׁלֵי שְׁלֹשָׁה אֲלָפִים רַבּוּ לָעָם אֲשֶׁר
וְאֵלֶּה: חִידָה נְתוּנָה לְשׁוֹנוֹת: פְּרוּטָה בְּאַחַת עֶשְׂרִים
בָּחַר מִשְׁבְּעִים לְשׁוֹנוֹת חֲסַלְתָּם מִשִּׁבְעִים בְּאָצְבַּע
רָשָׁתָם: וְגַם בְּשֵׁם פָּרַחִים כְּרוּבִים מֵאַצְבַּע יִשְׁבְּעוּ
אֱלֹהִים בְּמַעֲשֵׂה אָדוֹן: קֵל דֶּרֶךְ דֶּרֶךְ בְּרוּךְ יִקְרָאוּ
אַחֲרִית בְּשֵׁם קָדְשׁוֹ וְעַמּוֹ בָּחַר מִשְׁבְּעִים: יִקְרָא
שְׂמוֹת שִׁבְעִים וְעַמּוֹ בָּחַר מִשְׁבְּעִים וְשָׁמוֹ מַעֲלָה
לְמַעֲלָה מִשְׁבְּעִים בְּשַׁבְּנִים וּכְמִזְמוֹרוֹת

עצעמען אונ דיין שטן אונ דאם גליק אונ שׂל דאם זיינען אונים זיין
צוואקטא הערליכן און קעריגדער דיאך עקיגד ריזא דאך זיינען פיעל
צוי הערליכן אוייגדער דיא קריזען דיא שטעל פיען מענטשען מאך כבוד
יא נעמעעגם מינים דער אייגענוב נעפעגן שריעען דיעם שיון הערן
כעשעמערטע אונם ארבייל טעף טען (יענעגוב) אונד דיר דיי אייגעלונגם ינר זיך
נעל דיר ריזער כל רום ד נעפעלם: אומאר שרער אינדר גאם נעבעטשיונען
דין פירוש אן יא טעבר שנען גענענ יער איזאעער טרדה קרעטעג אונ יעדר
סינוש: יא ווא טעז אויאיא צור דאם רעם זיי נעציוטסען זיך דיו טרף אונ טעלר אין
דאם דיר זיינענ טוב טען גינעפא בטעל יע דע רעם פיעלא אונ אים פאר
דאם זיוגענ דרום אונישש טען ווערקא דיא בראכא אונד רעם ווערקען פא
אלהים בעאמטטעל זיינר דוד) עצר מייגע אום אלענוב דער פאר
ראם מם אויאים אוייא יא דיא טרף נעמן זיך קרף דיר דיר אונד מיט אום
סינואה: נאםפם מיום יער כלא ראם נעל איבערלענעל אפלקטר ה' אוממיוכש
דום עמער יורדם: יא ווא נעפעל פל כעיא קרף דיר דיר אונער נעטן אן אוטשען
ראם יע איר (דער תורה) אפיגע דע ראם זיין מעף מא וידר סיני אונ
יעגעא איר דוד ריוד ה' דר לאם שרד דם דודד סים פי גער מיודגל אינ
מינע געמענבען אונם ארבייט דע ראם דיר יערא אונ רעם יער נשמעל ווער
דאם יא זיונעל הייליגים ראם עם איבער עם ווארד זעף שיערם אונה פיר ביי
אום עשאפל זיינר דיא קעלינער טעלט רעם ראם נעכעל ראם בעגענער זע
שמואל, דיא ראם סעם נעגעצלינעגע קרף ראם נעכען קר פער נעבר
פיירמעעעגטבסראל.

Guarded Walls Rise

For the Jewish people confined within them, ghettos became places of immense suffering. Starvation was widespread and overcrowding was pervasive. In larger ghettos, huge numbers of people were forced to co-exist in a fraction of the space that

they had lived in before the war. Warsaw and Łódź were home to the two largest Jewish communities in pre-war Poland, and became the cities that contained the two largest ghettos. In Warsaw, 30 per cent of the city's population was forced into 2 per cent of its space. Here, as elsewhere, housing provision was so poor that several people were forced to share small rooms in apartments inhabited by multiple families. In spite of the appalling conditions, residents attempted to retain a degree of communal life however they could. They produced music and plays, organised children's education and attempted to continue religious practice. They were, however, ultimately unable to address the most fundamental issues affecting their lives.

Food supplies were completely insufficient to feed all ghetto residents, which led to the development of smuggling and black markets to fill the gap. In sealed ghettos, children small enough to escape through holes in the ghetto walls would smuggle food for their families, or work with larger networks in exchange for extra provisions. In some places, particularly in Warsaw, these activities thrived – and were even tacitly accepted by the Jewish councils.

Alongside the reality of starvation was the constant threat of disease. Epidemics ravaged ghetto populations. The conditions in which people were forced to live hastened the spread of infections and illnesses such as typhus, tuberculosis and dysentery. In the cold winter months the lack of heating and adequate clothing made people even more susceptible to deadly conditions.

Ghetto Tourism

Ghettos became sight-seeing destinations for members of the German military stationed in occupied Poland. Most had signs warning that entry for soldiers was forbidden, but in practice these were widely ignored. Senior Nazis were concerned that German troops entering the ghettos risked contracting diseases such as typhus. Despite rules forbidding it, the men visiting ghettos frequently took photos, and sometimes even film, of what they witnessed. The number of visitors grew as conditions in the ghettos worsened, with many focusing their attention on the scenes at the cemeteries.

For Historical Purposes

From the earliest days of the ghettos, residents began work on
secret projects to document their experiences. Those compiling
these archives took enormous risks, knowing that the Nazis
would execute them if their documents were discovered. They
wanted future generations to use these accounts to learn what
had happened – and understand the conditions in which they
had been forced to live. The archives were hidden in the hope
that one day they would be found and could speak for silenced
voices.

The *Oneg Shabbat* archive amassed in the Warsaw ghetto
was the largest such collection, growing to over 35,000 pages
of documentation. These were hidden in metal boxes and milk
containers and buried under buildings in the ghetto. Alongside
accounts scribbled on scraps of paper by ghetto inhabitants were
official Nazi documents and even reels of camera film.

CHAPTER FIVE

Massacre

On 22 June 1941, Hitler launched a major invasion of the Soviet Union, Germany's former ally. This attack, codenamed Operation 'Barbarossa', had long been central to Hitler's vision. He believed that securing *Lebensraum* (living space) in the east was essential for Germany's future. After initially making swift progress, the German advance was slowed. Strong Soviet resistance and the bitter reality of fighting on such a massive front took Hitler by surprise. When the Soviets prevented the Germans from reaching Moscow, the two sides became locked in a brutal stalemate.

Hitler wanted Germany's invasion of the Soviet Union to be a 'war of annihilation'. As his armies advanced east, they were followed by four SS execution units called *Einsatzgruppen A*, *B*, *C* and *D*. These task forces operated under the authority of Heinrich Himmler and massacred civilians in the name of security. They were formed of men from the Nazi terror apparatus and supported by members of the German police, military and local auxiliaries.

The *Einsatzgruppen* were given instructions to kill communist leaders and functionaries, Jews in party or state positions and 'other radical elements'. Because the Nazis believed that all Jewish people fitted these categories, eventually they considered all Jews to be legitimate targets. At first, they only targeted men. Within weeks they began killing women and by mid-August they were murdering children. Roma were regularly identified as 'dangerous elements' and were also killed in the mass shootings. By the end of 1942, more than one million people had been murdered.

Surrounded by Assassins

The instructions passed down by SS leader Heinrich Himmler required a large number of willing killers. His *Einsatzgruppen* units and sub-units were led by highly educated men, many of whom had doctorates. They had been handpicked for their roles and were all committed Nazis. Before being sent to eastern Europe, the senior officers had been brought together at a training facility in Pretzsch, near Leipzig, to be given instructions by Heydrich. Once in eastern Europe they carried out their tasks with enthusiasm and initiative, often designing their own methods for mass murder.

Mobile execution units entered towns and villages across eastern Europe. On some occasions their arrival unleashed waves of antisemitic violence from local populations that they were able to either encourage or allow to unfold. On others, they issued

Opposite far left: Sustained propaganda claimed all Jews in the Soviet Union were Bolshevik communists. The Nazis described this as the 'Judeo-Bolshevik threat', emphasising it on posters at home and abroad. They used this imagined threat to justify their ruthless actions as necessary for Germany's survival. This German poster reads, 'Victory over Bolshevism and plutocracy means being freed from the Jewish parasite'.

Opposite: This Polish-language Nazi poster reads, 'Death to the Jewish-Bolshevik murderous plague'.

Above right: Members of the German Army also participated in massacres. For men like Anton Brahsch, the war was an ideological crusade. In this postcard sent to his uncle in Hamburg, Brahsch wrote, 'We will beat the enemy and slaughter the Jews wherever they are!' Not all soldiers shared Brahsch's views and a few even spoke out against the mass shootings.

instructions telling Jews in the locality that they needed to present themselves at a given place and time – usually early morning – for resettlement. The night before these round-ups *Einsatzgruppen* leaders held meetings with local auxiliaries, support staff and any other relevant parties to arrange details of the *Aktion* (action) that was to follow. When Jewish people arrived at the area where they had been told to present themselves, they were walked towards a designated murder site and taken in groups to be shot. The murderers fired at their victims at close range, often taking breaks for food and drinks from tables that had been set up nearby. They were assisted in mass shootings by large numbers of local participants.

Erich von dem Bach-Zelewski

Erich von dem Bach-Zelewski was from a military background. He excelled in the SS, reaching the post of Higher SS and Police Leader in 1941. While his wife and six children remained in Germany, von dem Bach-Zelewski moved to Belarus to oversee the operations of *Einsatzgruppe B*. He led by example and was personally present at many mass shootings, including those in Minsk and Mogilev. In February 1942 he was hospitalised by a nervous breakdown, but in July he retook his post. By the end of that year, his unit had killed at least 134,000 Jewish men, women and children.

Left: Men from the German police also participated in the massacres. This leather jacket was worn by an officer of the *Schutzpolizei*, a branch of the uniformed police. In Germany, the *Schutzpolizei* maintained public order and directed traffic. In eastern Europe, they took part in mass shootings. They were often so close to their victims that their uniforms became soaked with blood.

Orders to kill Jews came directly from the Reich Security Main Office (RSHA) in Berlin. *Einsatzgruppen* commanders submitted regular reports about their 'progress' to the RSHA. These documents were widely circulated to senior Nazis. Franz Stahlecker, who led *Einsatzgruppe A*, produced a map along with his report in which he proudly described Estonia as '*judenfrei*' (free of Jews).

Sites of Mass Murder

Babyn Yar Ravine
A few kilometres north of the Ukrainian capital of Kiev lay a deep, winding ravine that dominated the local landscape. Known as Babyn Yar – or grandmother's ravine – it was a popular playground for the city's children. Locals went there to enjoy the scenery while younger family members splashed in its little stream.

29–30 SEPTEMBER 1941
On the morning of *Yom Kippur*, traditionally the holiest day of the Jewish year, nearly 34,000 of Kiev's Jews were assembled by *Einsatzgruppe C*. Most were women and children. They were marched to Babyn Yar, a place where 100 Roma had been killed just days before. On arrival they were made to undress and taken to the bottom of the ravine. Each group was forced to lie on the bodies of those that had been killed before them and then shot.

The Town of Chişinău

After the First World War, Chişinău (previously Kishinev) rapidly developed into an important commercial and industrial hub in Romania. Its professional opportunities attracted a large Jewish population, despite growing antisemitism. By the 1920s there were 77 synagogues and prayer halls in the city.

1 AUGUST 1941

On a summer's day in Chişinău's recently established ghetto, 450 starving young men and women volunteered for labour. They had been deceived into thinking they would be given food in exchange for work. In the intense heat they were marched to a large anti-tank ditch in the nearby village of Visterniceni. The men carried boxes containing what they thought were tools, but which actually contained ammunition. Romanian soldiers assisting *Einsatzgruppe D* used this ammunition in the massacre that followed. The women were shot first, then the men.

Šķēde beach

On hot summer days, local families from the bustling port city of Liepāja headed to the nearby beaches on Latvia's west coast. They relaxed on the nearby sandy seashore that stretched along its coastline. They enjoyed sunbathing, building sandcastles and kayaking in the Baltic Sea.

15–17 DECEMBER 1941

Across three freezing winter days, 4,000 of Liepāja's Jews – mainly women and children – were taken from their homes to the nearby fishing village of Šķēde. They were made to undress in the biting wind and led to the edge of a sand dune. While elderly women and children kept their underwear on, young women were forced to strip completely. Facing the Baltic Sea and with their backs to their German and Latvian executioners, they were shot.

Lubny Ravine

Standing on the banks of the River Sula, Lubny is one of Ukraine's oldest cities. It rapidly expanded after 1901 when a new railway linked it to other towns and cities. Factories manufacturing products such as tobacco and rope sprung up among its traditional buildings as the city's industries grew.

16 OCTOBER 1941

In the early morning, over 1,000 Jews from Lubny and the surrounding area gathered after receiving 'resettlement orders' from the German Army. They were assembled into columns and told they were being taken to a nearby village. On the way to their supposed destination, they were led to an isolated waiting area. From there, they were taken in small groups to a nearby ravine in front of a rope factory and shot. Their murderers were men from *Einsatzgruppe C*, supported by German policeman and local collaborators.

Ponary Forest

During the hot Lithuanian summers, people flocked to the small rural village of Ponary to escape the bustle of the nearby capital city, Vilnius. Walking in the scenic pinewood forest picking mushrooms and berries offered a relaxing contrast to urban life. Vilnius was known as the 'Jerusalem of Lithuania' for its thriving Jewish community.

11 JULY 1941

A few weeks after the German invasion, Jewish men in Vilnius were assembled by *Einsatzgruppe B* and Lithuanian police and marched to Ponary forest. On arrival they were made to undress and hand over valuables. They were then taken to pre-dug pits and shot. Gunfire from the killings was heard into the evening across the area. By the end of July, 5,000 working-age men had been killed at the site. In the months to come, women and children would follow.

Zvi-Dov and Rivka Abramovitz

Rivka and Moshe Abramovitz had a three-year-old son, Zvi-Dov. He was the first grandchild for Mordechai and Tova and the centre of the world for them and his Aunt Sara and Uncle Ze'ev. The family could trace their history in Lithuania back 300 years and were well respected in Raseiniai. This history was torn apart when *Einsatzgruppe A* entered the city in the summer of 1941. Zvi-Dov and Rivka were among a group of Jews taken to Kurpiškės forest in August and killed.

Shabtai Sonenson

The Betar Zionist youth movement was hugely important to Shabtai Sonenson. He became leader by 1941 and represented his hometown of Eyshishok at various Zionist-led activities. He taught Hebrew to help prepare adults for emigration to Palestine. Shabtai wanted to move there himself, but did not want to leave his family and friends behind. Germans occupied his town in June 1941. On 21 September, he was in a round up carried out by men from *Einsatzgruppe A*, taken to a local Jewish cemetery and shot.

Edik Tonkonogi

In the spring of 1941, seven-year-old Edik was living with his grandparents in Satanov, Ukraine. His parents were travelling with their Russian theatre group. Edik missed them and wrote to them frequently. His grandparents doted on him, giving him homemade cakes and *korijkis* (Russian milk cookies) when he came in from playing. He ate so many that in a letter, his grandmother told his mother that he had put on weight. In 1942, Edik and his grandparents were rounded up by *Einsatzgruppe C* alongside many of their neighbours and killed.

Opposite: Edik Tonkonogi's last letter to his parents ended, 'I kiss and hug both of you very tight...'

ДОРОГИЕ ПАПОЧКА
И МАМОЧКА: СЕВОДНЯ
ЦЭЛЫЙ ДЕНЬ ИДЕТ
ДОЖДЬ.Я ИГРАЮСЬ
ВИТЕЙ И С ГРИШКОЙ
ЦЭЛУЮ ВАС
ОЧЭНЬ КРЭПКО
ВАШ
ЭДИК.

CHAPTER SIX

Policy

T he Nazis had always imagined a world without Jews. Towards the end of 1941 this intention developed into a co-ordinated programme of mass murder across Europe.

Although Hitler had repeatedly claimed that Germany's future relied on eliminating 'the Jews', he had never been clear on how this should be achieved. Most of his regime's earlier policies had concentrated on forcing Jewish people out of Nazi territory, but as the war continued, its approach became increasingly more radical. The *Einsatzgruppen's* mass shootings of Jewish people on the Eastern Front had represented a murderous new phase for the Nazi regime, tipping their ideology and rhetoric over into virtually unbridled slaughter. From 1942 this was consolidated into a sweeping policy of centralised killing on a massive scale.

There was no single order from Hitler commanding the murder of Europe's Jews. Instead, he and members of his inner circle made a series of decisions in late 1941 and early 1942 that led to the programme of annihilation. From then on, what Hitler intended was clear to everyone involved. The policy developed in stages. Jews in occupied Poland were targeted first, before the programme spread to all parts of Nazi-occupied Europe and Germany's allies. Hitler and his inner circle were at the centre of this process, but they did not act alone.

Opposite: The view onto Lake Wannsee from the villa. A promotional brochure advertised 'completely refurbished guest rooms, a music room and games room (billiards), a large meeting room and conservatory, a terrace looking out onto the Wannsee, central heating, hot and cold running water, and all comforts' including 'good food, wine, beer and cigarettes.'

The Conference by the Lake

The 'final solution' was centrally controlled by the Reich Security Main Office (RSHA), run by Reinhard Heydrich.

The day-to-day management of deportations was overseen by Adolf Eichmann, head of the RSHA office responsible for 'Jewish affairs'. But this process required support and co-operation from individuals, organisations and government departments across German-controlled territory. On 20 January 1942, Reinhard Heydrich oversaw a high-level meeting to discuss the implementation of the 'final solution' in order to secure this support.

The meeting, which became known as the Wannsee Conference, was attended by 15 men representing agencies of both the state and the SS. Many were experienced civil servants and over half had doctorates in law. They discussed ways of co-operating on the mass murder and enslavement of Europe's Jews, alongside related issues such as classifications of people deemed *Mischlinge* (who had Jewish and non-Jewish parents or grandparents). Not all relevant organisations were present, however, and neither the military nor representatives of the German railways were invited – although both played a significant role as the programme evolved. This conference was not the moment when a policy of systematic murder was decided; no one present was senior enough to make those decisions – and anyway that process was already underway.

The meeting was held at a villa in Wannsee, an affluent suburb of Berlin. It was originally planned for 9 December 1941 but was rescheduled at short notice 'because of sudden events which... made it impossible'. These events were America's entry into the war and the launch of a major Soviet counter-offensive around Moscow. Attendees were invited to a 'discussion to be followed by breakfast'. The conversation lasted for around 90 minutes.

The Attendees

Reinhard Heydrich chaired the conference. The other attendees as listed on the minutes were:

Dr **Josef Bühler**, state secretary in the *Generalgouvernement*. Bühler represented Hans Frank and pushed for the 'final solution' to start in his territory.

Dr **Roland Freisler**, state secretary for the Ministry of Justice and a senior lawyer and judge. Freisler argued for radical measures for the treatment of people known as *Mischlinge*.

SS-*Gruppenführer* **Otto Hofmann**, head of the SS Race and Resettlement Main Office (RuSHA). Hofmann focused on the 'Germanisation' of Nazi-occupied territory in the east. His main interest was the categorisation of people known as *Mischlinge* and the policy of sterilisation.

SA-*Oberführer* Dr **Gerhard Klopfer**, state secretary for the Nazi Party Chancellery. Klopfer represented the head of the Chancellery Martin Bormann. The office he represented was central to the implementation of the 'final solution'.

Ministerialdirektor **Friedrich Wilhelm Kritzinger**, deputy head of the Reich Chancellery. Kritzinger was a career civil servant who worked for the office that co-ordinated legislation. He addressed the legal categorisations of people who were defined as Jews or 'half-Jews'.

SS-*Sturmbannführer* Dr **Rudolf Lange**, commander of the SD for Latvia. Lange was a commander in *Einsatzgruppen A* and was one of the only members of the conference who had direct personal experience of the mass murder of Jews.

Reichsamtleiter Dr **Georg Leibbrandt**, head of the political department of the Reich Ministry for the Occupied Eastern territories (RMO). Leibbrandt attended the conference to assist his superior Alfred Meyer and was interested in opportunities for German colonialism in eastern Europe.

Martin Luther, foreign ministry liaison to the SS. Luther advised on encouraging complicity with deportations from countries occupied by — and allied to — Germany.

Gauleiter Dr **Alfred Meyer**, deputy to Alfred Rosenberg, minister for the Reich Ministry of the Occupied Eastern territories (RMO). Meyer wanted to prevent large deportations of Jews into the Occupied Eastern territories and was an outspoken advocate of mass murder as a 'final solution'.

Heinrich Müller, head of the Nazi secret police (the *Gestapo*) and chief of department IV in the Reich Security Main Office (RSHA). Müller headed the department with overall responsibility for the implementation of the 'final solution'.

Erich Neumann, director of the Office of the Four-Year Plan. Neumann attended the conference as a representative of Hermann Göring. He was concerned about the impact of the plans for mass murder on the Four-Year Plan and argued that Jews employed in war industries should not be deported until suitable replacements for them were found.

SS-*Oberführer* Dr **Karl Eberhard Schöngarth**, member of the SD and commander of the RSHA field office in the *Generalgouvernement*. He was at the centre of a power struggle between different organisations about control of the 'final solution' in the *Generalgouvernement*.

Dr **Wilhelm Stuckart**, state secretary for the Ministry of the Interior. Stuckart attended the conference to represent Minister of the Interior Wilhelm Frick. He was an author of the 1935 Nuremberg Race Laws and argued for forced sterilisation rather than extermination.

SS-*Obersturmbannführer* **Adolf Eichmann**, head of Office IV B4 of the *Gestapo*, the office for 'Jewish affairs'. Eichmann arranged the conference on Heydrich's instructions and prepared the minutes.

On Behalf of the *Führer*

Adolf Hitler was at the centre of German decision-making. He established a group of senior Nazis around him who took responsibility for implementing his demands. Hitler only issued verbal directions to this loyal group, wanting to ensure that decisions relating to his murderous anti-Jewish policies could not be traced to him directly. Although instructions always came from Hitler, the inner circle was entrusted to decide how they were carried out. Within this network of trusted advisers there were ongoing conflicts and struggles for power and influence.

Hitler established the Obersalzberg, in the Bavarian Alps, as a second seat of government. He entertained both senior party members and international visitors — as well as their partners and children — in his house, the Berghof.

Hitler's partner, Eva Braun, captured many of these visits on film. It is likely that important conversations about the development of the Nazis' policy of annihilation were held at this location.

Top row: Martin Bormann *(left)* was Hitler's secretary. He controlled access to Hitler and passed on his verbal orders.

Joseph Goebbels developed the Nazi regime's propaganda to try and secure support for extreme anti-Jewish measures.

Eva Braun was Hitler's partner. She was deeply loyal to Hitler, but had no political ambition of her own.

Second row: Albert Speer led armaments and munitions production from 1942, using millions of slave labourers to support Germany's war effort.

Joachim von Ribbentrop was Hitler's foreign minister. He tried to persuade Germany's Axis partners to deport their Jewish populations.

Gerda Bormann was a fanatical Nazi married to Martin Bormann. The couple named their first child Adolf, after his godfather.

Third row: Anni Brandt was a famous swimmer in the 1920s. She was married to Karl Brandt and a strong supporter of Nazi racial policies.

Wilhelm Brückner was Hitler's chief adjutant. He supervised Hitler's personal staff and was one of his closest confidants.

Heinrich Himmler *(left)* had overall responsibility for the implementation of the policy to eliminate Europe's Jews. Reinhard Heydrich *(second from left)* was chief of the Reich Security Main Office (RSHA) and a key architect of the 'final solution'. Ernst Kaltenbrunner *(far right)* succeeded Heydrich in this role.

Bottom row: Julius Schaub *(left)* was Hitler's fiercely loyal personal assistant. He managed Hitler's day-to-day life.

Christa Schroeder was one of Hitler's personal secretaries. She was one of the few people Hitler tolerated criticism from.

Karl Brandt was Hitler's doctor and one of the leaders of the Nazi 'euthanasia programme' targeting disabled people.

CHAPTER SEVEN

Annihilation

From the start of 1942, the Nazis began the co-ordinated annihilation of Jews across Europe. These plans were carried out through a network that stretched over thousands of miles. Millions of people were selected for deportation and for death. Most were sent to be murdered in newly created killing centres in occupied Poland. Those not chosen for immediate death were enslaved in concentration camps. The Nazis' criteria for deciding who should be killed at once and who should be worked to death changed constantly – usually determined by the course of the war.

The programme of mass killing was accompanied by a programme of mass theft. Railway carriages took people to their deaths and brought their belongings back towards the Reich. These belongings were processed by both SS and state departments. Civil servants sat at desks totalling up the value of the possessions and personal effects of murdered adults and children.

Implementing the 'final solution' depended on the co-operation and assistance of individuals and communities across Europe. Not all those involved shared the Nazis' beliefs or ideology, but participated nevertheless for a range of different reasons. Soldiers, police officers, civil servants, doctors, lawyers, railway workers and countless others contributed to, or benefited from, the exploitation and murder of European Jews.

Trains carried deportees to ghettos, transit camps, concentration camps and killing centres. The Nazis incorporated these deportation transports into existing rail schedules. As the German military always took priority on the

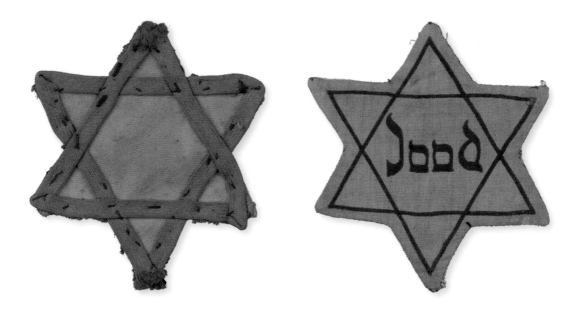

rail network, journeys were often delayed and people had to endure several days' confinement in crowded carriages. Where it was not practical to use railways for deportations, the Nazis also used boats and sometimes even cars. The lowest quality rail stock was allocated for these journeys, meaning that breakdowns were common.

By the end of 1943 the Nazis had murdered 4.8 million men, women and children.

Taking People Away

The Germans relied on European rail networks for mass deportations. The SS booked trains known as *Sonderzüge* (special trains) through the German state travel bureau. Train companies billed the SS for each 'passenger'. The SS usually demanded reimbursement for these transportation costs from the Jewish councils. Children under ten travelled at half price and those under four travelled for free. Journeys were made in appalling conditions, often on wagons designed for carrying freight and livestock.

Up to 100 people were crammed into sealed cars, which were heavily guarded. During the long journeys deportees usually had no access to fresh air, food or water. A single bucket was provided as the toilet for the whole carriage. The Nazis

Above: The Nazis forced Jewish adults and most children to wear an identifying badge or armband. From 1941, they made wearing the yellow star compulsory for Jews in Germany and most occupied territories. It marked people out for segregation and discrimination and made them easier to target during round-ups and deportations. Jewish people were usually forced to pay for the stars themselves.

Opposite top: In September 1942 the Nazis conducted a mass deportation from the Łódź ghetto to the Chełmno death camp. This *Aktion* mainly targeted children, the elderly and the sick. This photograph shows a child kissing a woman goodbye through the fence that separated deportees from those remaining in the ghetto.

Opposite bottom: Jewish ghetto police assisted in the process of deportation. They can be seen in this photograph walking alongside a column of people being sent from the Łódź ghetto to the Chełmno death camp.

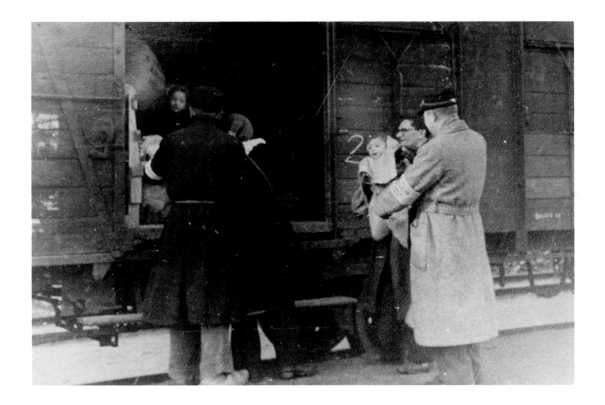

checked the names of those on each transport against a list.
Deportees were allowed to bring a single suitcase, a blanket
and enough food for three days of travel. Many did not
survive the journey.

Futures Lost

Deportees were told they were being 'resettled to the east' and
packed items they thought they would need for their new lives.
They were strongly encouraged to bring valuables and food,
but most of their choices were restricted by the strict limits they
were given about how much they were allowed to take.

People being deported had no information about the lives
they were supposedly destined for. Among the things they
packed were the practical objects they thought they would need
for day-to-day life. These included plates, bowls and cutlery
to eat with, and buttons, thimbles and thread to mend their
clothes. Among observant Jews, there were a large number of

items needed for religious practice. The Nazis' programme of sustained persecution led to some Jewish people questioning – or losing – their faith. For others, it became an important part of dealing with what was happening.

On the Edge of a Volcano

The Nazis began the systematic murder of people living in ghettos in March 1942. At first, those working – particularly in German war industries – were protected, but this was only temporary. The Germans instructed the *Judenräte* (Jewish councils) to draw up lists of people to be deported. Different policies were applied at ghettos in relation to the way this was managed, and as the process developed it became increasingly brutal. In the largest ghettos, the period of mass deportations went on for weeks and even months. Those selected for deportation were told to assemble at a holding area, and from there, they were taken to the trains. During the so-called *Grossaktion* in Warsaw that began on 22 July 1942, these trains left for Treblinka death camp twice a day for two months, carrying between five and six thousand people on each transport. By the end of 1943, most of the ghettos were empty.

Lost Lives

The Neumeyer Family

Photographs of Hans *(right)*, Vera and Ruth Neumeyer *(above)* and their family friend Julius Kohn *(above right)*. Hans and Vera were deported from Munich in the summer of 1942. Hans was sent to Theresienstadt and Vera probably to Auschwitz-Birkenau. Julius was deported to Auschwitz-Birkenau in early 1943. Hans and Vera's daughter, Ruth, had been sent to England on a *Kindertransport* before the war. In July 1942 she received a message from her mother that began with the words, 'Going on journey'. It would be the last message from her she received. Four months later a message from her grandfather confirmed that he no longer knew where her parents were.

The Wohl Family ⌄

The Wohl family were living in different parts of the world at the outbreak of war. In January 1943, parents Leonhard and Clara Wohl – who had been unable to escape – sent a last message to their daughters, who had found refuge in England. On 19 February, Leonhard and Clara were deported from Berlin to Auschwitz-Birkenau.

The Koniec Family ⌃

The Koniec family were separated when children Dori and Herbi departed for Britain on a *Kindertransport* in 1939. Parents Sigmund and Karoline Koniec were taken from their home in Bratislava to a camp at Žilina when deportations began from the Slovak Republic. In June 1942 they were transported to Auschwitz-Birkenau where they were killed. Their children, Dori and Herbi, received a message from a former neighbour informing them of their parents' deportation.

Settela Steinbach ∧
Anna Maria 'Settela' Steinbach was the daughter of a Sinti trader and violinist. In May 1944, Roma were targeted in a round-up across the Netherlands. The Steinbachs were taken to Westerbork transit camp and transported east, together with 244 other Sinti. A Jewish prisoner filming under orders captured this image of Settela as the train departed.

Marianne Grunfeld ‹
Marianne Grunfeld, Auguste Spitz and Therese Steiner were Jewish refugees living in Guernsey when the Germans occupied the Channel Islands in 1940. They were sent to occupied France in April 1942. On 20 July, they were forced to board a freight train that took them to Auschwitz-Birkenau — Marianne appears on this transport list. All three were killed.

Hermine Petschau ∨
Hermine Petschau was a 78-year-old Austrian woman living in Prague. In July 1942, she received this notice telling her that she was to be deported. She was instructed to report at the assembly point at 4pm on 13 July.

Lfd. Nr.	Name u. Vorname:	Geburtsdat. u. Ort:	Beruf:	Staatsangehörigkeit:	Wohnort:
28	Grumbacher Mini	6.7.97 Rust	ohne	Deutsch.R.	Chenehutte les Tuffaux
29	Grumbacher Rita	15.11.20 Freiburg	ohne	Deutsch.R.	Chenehutte les Tuffaux
30	Grün Juliette geb.Lorintz	19.9.03 Budapest	Näherin	Ungarn	Laval
31	Guthmann Edwige	9.6.02 Metz	ohne	Deutsch.R.	Le Mans
32	Gutmann Emma	5.5.00 Metz	ohne	Deutsch.R.	Le Mans
33	Herrman Mathilde geb.Chen	7.12.07 St.Mars aux Mines	ohne	Luxemburg	Chateau-Gontier
34	Honick Chanina	8.5.12 Feltyn	ohne	Polen	Chateau-Gontier
35	Honick Sluva geb.Muntz	28.4.22 Sambor	Schneiderin,	Polen	Chateau-Gontier
36	Horowitz Gerta	5.4.18 Wien	Studentin,	Oesterreich	La Ferté Bernard
37	Gotainer Susa geb.Warech	24.7.10 Lodz	ohne	?	Viniers
38	Grünfeld Marianne	5.12.12 Kattowitz	Arbeiterin,	Deutsch.R.	Laval
39	Jakubowiz Anna geb.Reichman	6.9.14 Polaniz	ohne	Polen	Paris
40	Kesler Anna geb.Sulim	14.7.96 Falticani	ohne	Rumänin	Le Mans
41	Kormorner Helena	30.8.25 Wien	ohne	Oesterreicher,	Morannes
42	Kormorner Therese geb.Becker	2.10.01 Berlin	ohne	Oesterreich.	Morannes

11.7.1942

Wir teilen Ihnen mit, dass Sie in den Transport AAr eingereiht wurden. Laut beiliegender amtlicher Vorladung haben Sie Montag, den 13.7.1942 um 16 Uhr am Messegelände anzutreten. Das Gepäck wollen Sie mit Name, Adresse und Buchstaben AAr bezeichnen, da Ihnen die Transportnummer erst auf dem Messegelände zugeteilt wird. Ihr Mitgepäck wird ab morgen früh von unserem Sammeldienst in Ihrer Wohnung abgeholt werden.

Beilagen

Jüdische Kultusgemeinde in ...
Židovská náboženská obec v ...

Sdělujeme Vám, že jste byl/a/ zařazen/a/ do transportu AAr. Podle přiloženého úředního vyzvání byl určen Vás ... up na pondělí, dne 13.7.1942 v 16 hod. odpoledne. Zavazadlo popište jménem, adresou a ... Anna jelikož transportní číslo Vám budou přiděleno teprve na shromaždišti. Vaše hlavní zavazadlo bude odvezeno naším sb ... mem službou během zítřejšího dne

Into Hiding

Some Jewish people tried to evade capture by living in hiding. This hiding took many forms. Some individuals were offered — or paid for — secret spaces in the homes of non-Jewish people; others were able to live in plain sight under false identities. Families were rarely able to stay together. Those in hiding witnessed the violent treatment of Jews while living under constant threat of discovery. Their chances of survival were extremely low.

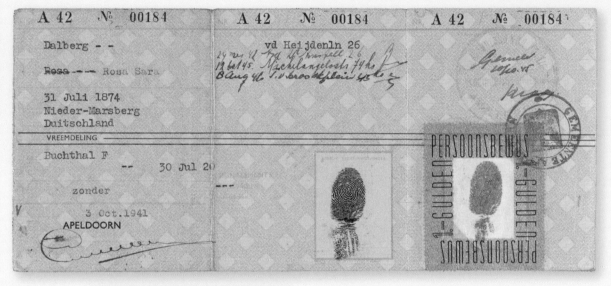

Some Jewish people in larger cities used forged papers to live in the open under false identities. These identity cards belonged to a German Jewish woman living in the Netherlands. One bears her real name, Rosa Dalberg-Buchthal, while the other carries her false identity, Anna van Driel.

Right: Anna Wiechec was a Polish widow living in Kraków. In 1943, she took in a Jewish woman and a five-year-old girl called Marysia. Each morning the pair left Anna's flat. When they returned each night, Marysia set the table with her silver spoon and fork – all that remained of her previous life. One day they left as usual, but never returned.

Prepared to Resist

On 19 April 1943, the Nazis entered the Warsaw ghetto to deport its remaining residents. Jewish resistance organisations responded by launching a long-planned armed uprising. After several weeks of fighting the uprising was defeated and the ghetto destroyed.

Georgy Halpern

Georgy Halpern was one of 44 young people sheltered in a home for refugee children in Izieu, France. He was eight years old. The orphanage was run by a Jewish welfare organisation. Georgy was happy in his new home but missed his parents. On 6 April 1944, he was with other children in the dining hall eating breakfast and drinking hot chocolate when the *Gestapo* stormed in. The children were rounded up and forced onto trucks that were waiting outside. They were sent hundreds of miles away to the transit camp at Drancy. From there, they were deported to Auschwitz-Birkenau and killed.

Far from Parents' Arms

Some children lived openly with non-Jewish families or in orphanages under false names. They usually had to adopt a Christian identity to help support their secret identity. Others lived in isolation, remaining physically concealed throughout the day in lofts, cellars or specially made hiding spaces. Their safety relied on complete secrecy from those around them. This secrecy was increasingly imperilled as the Nazis offered bribes and incentives for the reporting of people who were concealing Jews.

Opposite: Georgy was Julius and Serafine Halpern's only child. These family photographs were taken shortly before he was placed in the children's home in Izieu in an attempt to keep him safe.

Above: Georgy Halpern with other young residents at the home in Izieu.

Right: Georgy sent his parents letters describing his school lessons and adventures in the French countryside. He also sent them drawings of ships and castles.

The Righteous

Across Europe some individuals took enormous risks to help Jewish people. Although these rescuers were in the minority, their efforts saved thousands of lives. Some were driven by moral concerns, while others were motivated by money. Regardless of their reasons, anyone helping Jews knowingly endangered their own life. Rescue took many forms; some acts were individual initiatives but most involved complex operations run by resistance or underground networks. Rescuing a single person relied on the help of countless others.

Přemysl Dobiáš

Přemysl Dobiáš was part of a resistance group in Nazi-occupied Czechoslovakia. Members of the group smuggled Jews out to safe countries at great risk to themselves. Přemysl's involvement was discovered by the *Gestapo* and he was arrested in December 1941. He was tortured for information and imprisoned before being sent to Mauthausen concentration camp for nearly four years.

The Pernýs and the Gavalovičs

Vojtěch and Mária Perný and Helena and Viliam Gavalovič protected a Jewish family living in Nitra, Slovakia. They hid all eight family members in an empty flat in the apartment block where Vojtěch Perný was caretaker. The Pernýs and the Gavalovičs brought food to the family and warned them of imminent danger, ultimately saving them from deportation.

Leopold and Magdalena Socha

Leopold Socha worked for the sanitation department in Lwów. He helped Jews who took refuge in the sewers during the liquidation of the city's ghetto. Both Leopold and his wife Magdalena brought food, clothing — and even newspapers — to those hiding. They initially expected to be paid, but continued to assist when the money ran out.

Chiune Sugihara

Chiune Sugihara was a Japanese diplomat based in Kovno, Lithuania. He was ordered to leave when the Soviet Union annexed the country in June 1940. Chiune was greatly concerned about the plight of Jewish people in Europe. Against orders he issued up to 3,500 transit visas for Japan — and continued even as he boarded the train to leave.

Refik Veseli

Refik Veseli was a Muslim teenager who worked with Jewish photographer Moshe Mandil in Tirana, Albania. When the Germans invaded Albania in 1943, Refik's family protected the Mandil family. They brought them from Tirana to the Veseli's home village in the mountains and hid them there. Refik's brother Xhemal later brought a second Jewish family to join them.

Otto Weidt

Otto Weidt hired blind and deaf Jewish employees in his Berlin workshop making brooms and brushes. He went to extraordinary lengths to keep the people he employed safe from deportation, claiming the business's work was essential for the war effort. He succeeded until February 1943, when the *Gestapo* arrested most Jews still working in Berlin — including those in Otto's factory.

Opposite: Leopold Socha, a sanitation worker in Lwów who used his position to help hide Jews.

Above: Chiune Sugihara, Japanese Imperial consul posted in Lithuania.

Left: Otto Weidt, an opponent of the Nazis who used his workshop to try and protect German Jews.

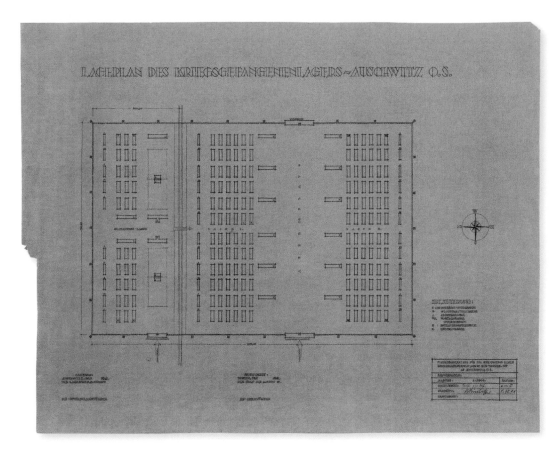

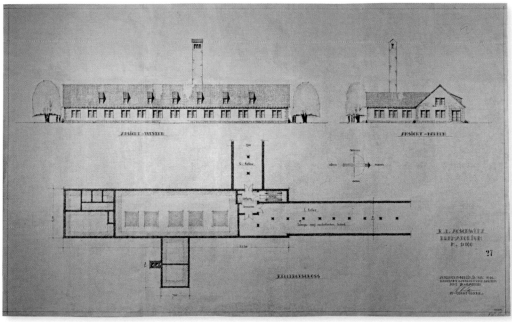

CHAPTER EIGHT

Killing Centres

A

Opposite: These designs show the plans for Auschwitz-Birkenau in October 1941. They were revised in 1942 as the arrangements for Auschwitz in the 'final solution' evolved. The new plans included four permanent gassing installations called 'crematoria'. This drawing of Crematoria II at Auschwitz-Birkenau was modified to include an undressing room and gas chamber, as well as ovens for corpse disposal.

t the end of 1941, the Nazis began to construct purpose-built death camps to kill people on a massive scale, using poison gas. These *Vernichtungslager* (extermination camps) were technically and administratively separate from the concentration camp system. The first became operational in December 1941 in Chełmno, near the Łódź ghetto. Three more opened from spring 1942 near the villages of Bełżec, Sobibór and Treblinka. These were located in occupied Poland and intended primarily – though not exclusively – to kill Jews from the area known as the *Generalgouvernement* (General Government).

Other death camps were built as attachments to existing concentration camps at Majdanek, Maly Trostenets and Auschwitz. The death camp at Auschwitz was called Auschwitz-Birkenau. Construction began there in autumn 1941. It was located about 1.5 miles from the main camp, Auschwitz I, and became both the centre of the Nazis' mass murder and enslavement of Jews across Europe and their biggest death camp. From 1943, as the other death camps began to close, the gas chambers in Auschwitz-Birkenau operated day and night.

The Nazis relied on speed, deception and violence to commit mass murder at their *Vernichtungslager*. SS men and auxiliary guards rushed new arrivals off the trains, telling them that they were at a midpoint on their journey. An officer standing on the arrival platform announced that showering was necessary before 'resettlement'. Men were separated from women and children and then everyone was forced to hurriedly undress. Some of those arriving from ghettos had heard rumours about what had been happening in these places, those coming from western Europe knew far less. Most were dead within hours of arrival.

The Murderers

The death camps were developed for a few different reasons. Senior Nazis were concerned that mass shootings were too inefficient – in respect of both the number of personnel required and bullets used – and too damaging for the mental health of the killers. They were also worried about the highly public nature of the shootings and how conspicuous they had become. By creating death camps in remote locations, using cheap materials, they hoped to address all of these issues. They based their approach to the construction of the death camps on experiences derived from both the 'euthanasia programme' and experiments with gas vans that some *Einsatzgruppen* had been conducting.

The development of the death camps of Belzec, Sobibor and Treblinka was placed under the control of SS officer Odilo Globočnik. Globočnik appointed experienced killers to run them – many of whom had experience of murdering disabled people by gas through working in the Nazis' 'euthanasia programme'. The technique used at the camps was developed following a series of experiments, but essentially relied on the use of motor engines to pipe carbon monoxide into sealed chambers. This method – and some of the processes of deception – had been developed in Chełmno towards the end of 1941. Here people were forced to undress in a building, before being driven into the back of a van that was parked up against the building and disguised as a separate room. The van had its exhaust fumes redirected into the rear compartment, so that those within it were asphyxiated as it was driven towards a burial pit.

The death camps were operated by a small number of SS officers who were supported by auxiliary guards known as 'Ukrainians' (though not all of them came from Ukraine). Between them, they killed thousands of people a day. These men were paid a bonus for their work, but had to agree to the strictest secrecy.

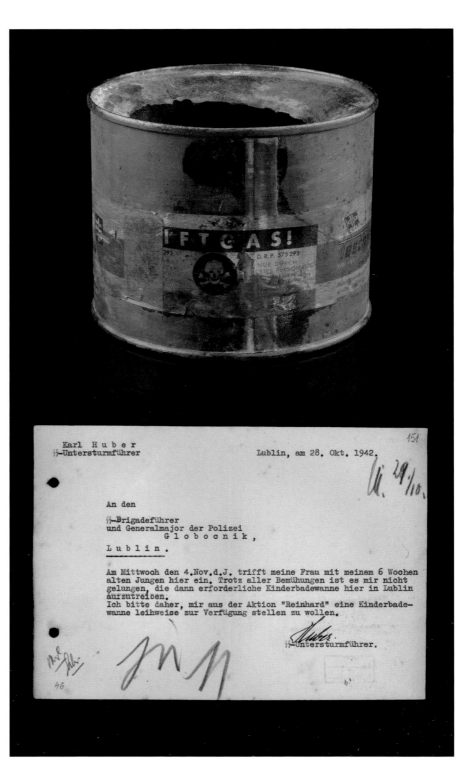

Top right: Unlike most of the other death camps, the SS at Auschwitz-Birkenau used hydrogen cyanide – sold as a commercial pesticide called Zyklon B – as the method of murder. Zyklon B was a product patented by Degesch and sold by Testa and Heli in Europe. Once the doors were locked, SS men emptied tins containing pellets coated with the substance into wire-framed columns through hatches in the ceiling. These became highly toxic on contact with the moist, warm air in the gas chambers. To maintain the pretence that the rooms were showers, the Nazis attached fake shower heads to the ceiling, though these were not plumbed in to anything.

Bottom right: SS officer Karl Huber wrote this letter to senior official Odilo Globočnik seeking a bathtub for his six-week-old son. Huber specifically requested an item from Operation 'Reinhard' – the code name for the murder of Jews in occupied Poland. Huber would have known he was asking for a bathtub belonging to a murdered child.

Guards drank and socialised within the camp and at bars in nearby towns. Over-consumption of alcohol was common, despite warnings against it from Heinrich Himmler. They maintained a ready supply of beer, wine and spirits which they supplemented with alcohol stolen from victims' luggage.

Odilo Globočnik headed Operation 'Reinhard', the plan to murder approximately 1.7 million Jews in occupied Poland. He received orders directly from SS leader Heinrich Himmler. Globočnik's personal instructions ensured the programme of mass murder was carried out at ferocious speed. He frequently boasted of his 'achievements' to other Nazis.

Hans-Heinz Schütt was a bookkeeper at Sobibor. He had previously worked in an administrative role in the 'euthanasia programme'.

At Sobibor he was also the 'cashier', handing people worthless 'receipts' in exchange for their money and valuables. Schütt was rarely violent, but played a key role in deceiving new arrivals and concealing the camp's true purpose.

Christian Wirth oversaw the construction and management of Belzec death camp. He used his experience in the Nazis' 'euthanasia programme' to devise the entire procedure for mass murder at Belzec. Wirth went on to manage the expansion and development of gas chambers at Sobibor and Treblinka. He was known as 'Wild Christian' and 'Christian the Terrible'.

Lorenz Hackenholt was considered a gassing expert because of his work in all six 'euthanasia' facilities.

He designed and operated the gas chambers at Belzec, using an engine from a Soviet tank to deliver the fatal carbon monoxide gas. The Nazis placed a satirical plaque above the building's door that read 'Hackenholt Foundation'.

Ernst Zierke supervised parts of the day-to-day murder operations at Belzec. As a nurse in Grafeneck and Hadamar euthanasia facilities, he had experience in state-organised killings. During his time in Belzec he worked on the unloading ramp, managed the undressing stage and tried to keep people calm so they entered the gas chambers without panicking.

Top right: Gestapo in Vienna sent this letter to the Head Office of Operation 'Reinhard' in Lublin. It requested clothes for 700 Polish people who the Nazis believed could be 'Germanised' (made into Germans). At the death camps, slave labourers removed yellow stars and any identifying marks from stolen clothing before it was redistributed. If any traces of the stars remained, the labourer responsible risked being executed.

Bottom right: This letter, marked as secret, requests '10 medium-sized suitcases' for two *Einsatzgruppen* mobile killing units. While murder with gas in death camps became the main method of Nazi mass murder from 1942, the *Einsatzgruppen*'s mass shootings continued. At the time this letter was written, ghettos in the Soviet Union were being emptied and the remaining Jews shot by *Einsatzgruppen* units.

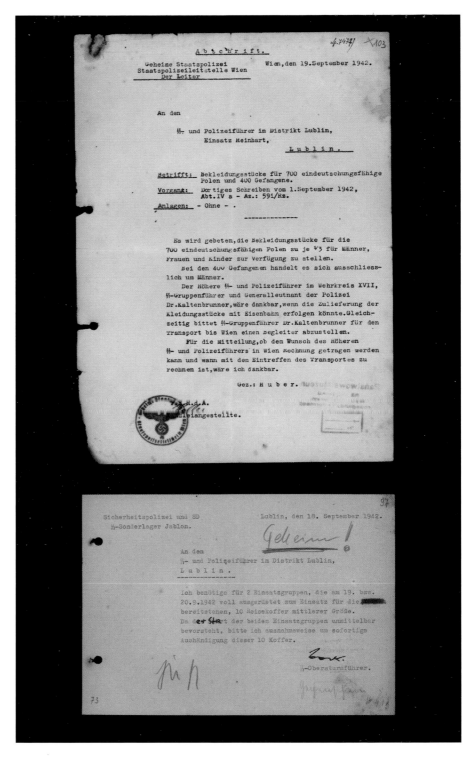

The Sole Witnesses

The SS kept a small number of Jewish men that they called the *Sonderkommando* (special squad) to assist in the murder process. After each gassing operation, the *Sonderkommando* had to enter the chamber and search the tangled bodies for hidden valuables and gold teeth before taking the corpses to be buried or burned. They then wiped blood and excrement from the gas chamber's walls and floor in preparation for the next transport. They sometimes encountered family and friends among the bodies that they were forced to carry, or drag with leather straps. The SS kept the *Sonderkommando* in a separate area within the death camps, in order to maintain secrecy. They executed them at semi-regular intervals, replacing them with men from new transports.

Strangled by Gas

The Nazis' use of deception was designed to make the process of mass murder as efficient as possible, and to reduce the chances of resistance. It was also intended to make the theft of valuables as straightforward as possible. The Nazis forced people to deposit money and jewellery with the 'cashier' before making them undress. In some camps, the 'cashier' gave them concrete tags as 'receipts', telling them to ensure they kept the tags safe so they could collect their valuables after their 'shower'. This maintained the illusion that those entering the chamber would live to see their belongings again. Young slave labourers walked among the crowd handing a strip of fabric to each person so they could tie their shoes together as a pair. People were told it would make the shoes easier to find after their shower – in reality it made it easier for the Nazis to redistribute them in the Reich.

At Belzec, the Nazis disguised the gas chambers as a 'Jewish bathhouse' with flowers and the Star of David at the entrance. They sometimes handed people soap and even towels. Women

were told they needed their hair cut for disinfection, before having their heads shorn with blunt scissors. After their murder, this hair was sent to Germany and used in the manufacture of industrial felt. At Treblinka, the floors had red tiles procured from a large Polish ceramics manufacturer under the control of the German occupiers and the walls of the rooms had small beige tiles covering the lowest two thirds. The doors were made of steel and insulated with rubber. As people filed into the chambers, they were told to put their hands in the air in order to allow as many people to fit in as possible.

Neither the Zyklon B used at Auschwitz-Birkenau and Majdanek nor the carbon monoxide gas used at other death camps worked instantly. Those sealed inside the chambers were subject to an agonising death. When the doors were opened, the bodies of loved ones were often found gripping each other so tightly that they could not be pulled apart.

Deprived of Everything

For many people, the murder of Europe's Jews was a lucrative business. Before being killed, Jews were stripped of their belongings. Their food was taken by those working in the camps and their clothes were redistributed by several charities to Germans across the Reich. Their valuables were taken by the state. Camp guards became rich by keeping jewellery and money for themselves – despite strict rules prohibiting it. Himmler considered this to be the antithesis of the values he expected from SS men, and those caught doing it risked being thrown out of the organisation or even being put in concentration camps themselves. As knowledge about what was happening in the death camps developed, residents from nearby towns and villages traded and bartered stolen goods, and local economies grew.

The World Watches On

Information about the wide-scale murder of Europe's Jews began to filter out of occupied Europe in the spring and summer of 1942. Many people found the fragments of information difficult to make sense of and impossible to believe. On 17 December 1942, the Allies issued a joint declaration condemning the Germans' murderous policies and threatening them with punishment once the war was over. In an unprecedented move, a minute's silence was held in the British parliament. No further action was taken.

Szmul Zygielbojm

Szmul Zygielbojm was one of two Jewish representatives on the National Council of the Polish government-in-exile in London. Through his contacts in the Bund and the Polish resistance, he received detailed information about the tragedy unfolding in Europe. He lobbied ceaselessly for officials to intervene on behalf of Polish Jews. Eventually, in May 1943, in protest at what he called 'the inaction in which the world watches and permits the destruction of the Jewish people', he took his own life.

The Allied governments maintained that the best way to help was to win the war as quickly as possible, but a vocal minority in Britain and the United States clamoured for immediate action as news of the extermination of Jews in Europe grew. In June 1942, the *Daily Telegraph* published one of the first articles about the extermination of Polish Jews. They used information supplied by Szmul Zygielbojm, a member of the Polish government-in-exile as the basis for their report. In general the press carried inconsistent coverage of Nazi atrocities against Jews throughout the war. Few newspapers gave much space to such reports and those that did rarely made it front page news.

Gerhart Riegner was the World Jewish Congress (WJC) representative in Switzerland. In August 1942, he sent messages to colleagues in Britain and America after receiving information about Nazi plans to murder millions of Jews. This information confirmed the rumours about a systematic programme of murder. British MP and WJC representative Samuel Silverman sent a telegram with Riegner's message to Rabbi Stephen Wise, a prominent Jewish Leader in the United States. Riegner's information was initially viewed with scepticism and the US State Department asked that its contents be kept secret until they were verified. It was eventually released to the press by Rabbi Wise on 24 November 1942. The information appeared in hundreds of newspapers the next day.

Zieken-rapport.

CHAPTER NINE

Enslavement

As the war continued, the Nazis' intention to murder Europe's Jews was increasingly at odds with Germany's urgent need for workers. Their war production was being massively outpaced by that of the Allies and their armed forces were struggling under heavy losses. Facing desperate demand for workers to make armaments, the Nazis resorted to using prisoners in concentration camps as disposable slave labour in the factories.

The concentration camp network had undergone a constant process of reinvention since its first establishment in the early days of the Nazi regime. New camps had opened and closed and by the outbreak of war, Dachau was the only *Konzentrationslager* or KL (concentration camp) still operating from the regime's first two years. The war drove a rapid expansion of the network – particularly from 1942. This period of expansion transformed both its scale and its reach.

In March, Himmler decided that the concentration camps should be placed under the control of the SS *Wirtschafts-Verwaltungshauptamt* or WVHA (Main Economic and Administrative Office). This decision led to fundamental changes to their size and composition as they were adapted to accommodate the huge volume of prisoners who were now forcibly placed into the service of Germany's war effort. The expansion was achieved by both increasing capacity in existing camps and also building new ones. In September 1942 there were 110,000 prisoners in concentration camps; 11 months later that number had risen to 224,000 and by December 1945 the total prisoner population had ballooned to over 714,000.

These men and women were held in 24 main concentration camps and thousands of sub-camps.

The increase in the number of prisoners in the camps was driven in part by the introduction of Jewish people into the system. At the start of 1942 there were relatively very few Jewish people in concentration camps – some 5,000 at most – but by 1944 this number had risen to hundreds of thousands. Even camps in parts of the Reich that the Nazis had proudly declared as *Judenfrei* (Jew free) years earlier now housed Jewish prisoners.

Despite the increased number of Jews within the network, concentration camps remained completely peripheral to the personal experiences of the majority of Jewish people targeted by the Nazis. By the time Himmler determined that Jews should be enslaved within the KL system in large numbers, millions had already been killed in mass shootings or in death camps – and hundreds of thousands more had died through starvation and disease in the ghettos. From 1942, the concentration camp system began increasingly to intersect with Nazi anti-Jewish persecution. However, for most of Europe's Jews, this was not where this persecution either began or ended.

As the focus of concentration camps became more and more centred on slave labour, prisoners' survival relied – at least in

Opposite top: Leibisch Engelberg was given this jacket during his time as a labourer in concentration camps.

Opposite bottom: Jan Imich's jacket.

Leibisch Engelberg	Leibisch Engelberg, his wife Liebe and two young sons David and Israel were interned in France in August 1942. Less than two weeks later they were among 1,000 Jews crammed onto the arrivals platform at Auschwitz-Birkenau. Leibisch, who was relatively young and healthy, was selected for labour. His family were sent to the gas chambers.
Jan Imich	Jan Imich was arrested at the age of 14 while in hiding with a non-Jewish family. He was imprisoned and subjected to medical experimentation before entering the concentration camp system. His mother was deported to Belzec and killed. Jan was forced to carry coal to keep the crematoria burning at Mittelbau-Dora concentration camp. One day a guard saw him bending down to pick up some potato peel. The guard beat him with a baton, causing permanent damage to Jan's hearing.

Zentralstelle für jüdische
Auswanderung Amsterdam.
Adema v.Scheltemaplein 1.
   Telefoon 97001.

           O P R O E P I N G

                              L   31 No. 2.

       U moet zich voor eventueele deelname aan een, onder politie-
toezichtstaande, werkverruiming in Duitschland voor persoonsonderzoek
en geneeskundige keuring naar het doorgangskamp Westerbork, station
Hooghalen, begeven.

       Daartoe moet U op 30 Juli 1942 om 17.— uur op de verzamel-
plaats R'dam Entrepotstr. Loods 24 aanwezig zyn.

       Als bagage mxmxtxM mag medegenomen worden :

              1 koffer of rugzak
              1 paar werklaarzen
              2 paar sokken
              2 onderbroeken
              2 hemden
              1 werkpak
              2 wollen dekens
              2 stel beddengoed (overtrek met laken)
              1 eetnap
              1 drinkbeker
              1 lepel en
              1 pullover
              handdoek en toiletartikelen.

en eveneens marschproviand voor 3 dagen en de voor die tyd geldende
distributiekaarten.

       De mee te nemen bagage moet in gedeelten gepakt worden.

   a. Noodzakelyke reisbehoeften.
       daartoe behooren: 2 dekens, 1 stel beddegoed, levensmiddelen
       voor 3 dagen, toiletgerei, etensbord, eetbestek, drinkbekere,

   b. Groote bagage.
       De onder b. vermelde bagage moet worden gepakt in een stevige
       koffer of rugzak, welke op duidelyke wyze voorzien moet zyn
       van naam, voornamen, geboortedatum en het woord " Holland ".
       Gezinsbagage is niet toegestaan.
       Het voorgaande moet nauwkeurig in acht genomen worden, daar de
       groote bagage in de plaats van vertrek afzonderlyk ingeladen
       wordt. De verschillende bewys- en persoonspapieren mogen niet
       by de bagage verpakt worden, doch moeten, voor onmiddellyk ver-
       toon gereed, medegedragen worden.
       De woning moet ordelyk achtergelaten en afgesloten worden, de huis-
       sleutels moeten worden medegenomen.
       Niet medegenomen mogen worden ; levend huisraad.

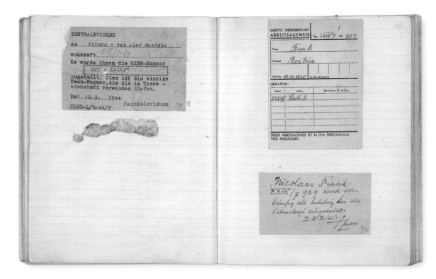

Opposite: This set of instructions was given to Dutch Jews who were being sent to Westerbork.

Right: Beatrix Frank and her three sons were among 4,924 Dutch Jews deported from Westerbork to Theresienstadt. Most Dutch Jews were sent directly from Westerbork to Auschwitz-Birkenau or Sobibor. Beatrix was issued with this work card after securing employment in the laundry at Theresienstadt. Her job enabled her to secretly wash herself and her sons in hot water.

part – on their productivity. In 1941, the Nazis had broadened their 'euthanasia programme' to include concentration camp prisoners. This policy (codenamed '*Aktion 14f13*') ordered that prisoners unable to work should be sent to 'clinics' that had been used in the programme for execution. This led to ongoing prisoner 'selections' and brought the concentration camp system firmly into the Nazis' network of mass murder. As this suggests, the decision to begin introducing Jewish people into the concentration camps did not represent a different 'solution' to the Jewish question, only a different way of achieving it. When Jewish slave labourers became too exhausted, malnourished or ill to be considered productive, they were murdered. Even those who were 'fit to work' were sometimes killed – and mass murders in gas chambers continued. The complete annihilation of Jews remained the Nazis' main goal.

Auschwitz

The Nazis' decision to exploit Jewish people for slave labour within the concentration camp system drove Auschwitz increasingly to the centre of Jewish policy. Originally conceived and operated as a camp to hold Polish political prisoners, it underwent a period of uneven development through 1942 as its purpose was redefined. While Auschwitz would still be used as

a camp to hold various categories of prisoners, it was to become a focal point of the 'final solution' and a centre of both slave labour and mass killing. Jewish people were deported there from across Nazi-occupied and Nazi-allied Europe. Most were sent directly to Birkenau, the largest of its three main camps. On arrival they were subject to a selection process by the SS. While the majority were killed in gas chambers, those considered 'fit to work' were kept alive – though only temporarily. They were either held at Birkenau or at one of Auschwitz's many smaller sub-camps, or were sent to other concentration camps across occupied Europe.

Gateways

In western Europe the Nazis created a series of transit camps. They used these as centralised collection points to hold people temporarily before 'resettling' them to death camps and concentration camps in the east. Drancy, in a suburb of Paris, became the major transit camp for Jews in France, with deportations beginning in 1942 – usually to Auschwitz-Birkenau. In the Netherlands there were transports every Tuesday morning carrying Jews and Roma from Westerbork transit camp to the Auschwitz-Birkenau and Sobibor death camps. Converted military barracks in Mechelen, between Antwerp and Brussels, housed Jews in Belgium before they were deported to Auschwitz-Birkenau. Theresienstadt, a ghetto in occupied Czechoslovakia that also operated as a transit camp, became a destination for Jews from Germany, Austria, the Netherlands and Czechoslovakia. Many thousands were deported from there to the death camps, particularly Auschwitz-Birkenau. Unlike concentration camps, some transit camps were run by local collaborators and not the SS.

Opposite clockwise from top:
A red stripe and the letters
KL (*Konzentrationslager*,
concentration camp) were
painted on the back of this
jacket issued to a prisoner in
Majdanek.

Securing footwear was
critical to prisoners'
survival. The crude wooden
clogs issued by camp
authorities were heavy and
uncomfortable. They were
usually ill-fitting, leading to
blisters and cuts that could
easily become infected in
the filthy conditions. Despite
this, clogs offered at least
a little protection and were
better than no shoes at all.

Prisoners found without
their cap could be killed. SS
guards sometimes amused
themselves by throwing
a prisoner's cap towards
the perimeter fence and
shooting them as they
retrieved it. During roll calls
prisoners had to remove
their caps on demand. They
were expected to do this in
complete unison and were
beaten if they failed to do so.

Camps in Communities

As the concentration camp network vastly expanded, from 1943 thousands of sub-camps sprang up from the main camps. These were usually established near weapons and aircraft factories or construction sites and varied widely in terms of size and conditions. Sub-camps were overseen by the main camps, but were often operated by private businesses. They were an opportunity for the SS to support the war effort and make money. By 1944, they appeared in almost all towns and cities across the Reich. As this process unfolded, concentration camp prisoners became an increasingly conspicuous presence throughout German territory.

A Living Death

Concentration camp prisoners were subjected to ongoing physical and psychological torment. New arrivals had their hair shaved before being forced through showers that were typically scalding hot or freezing cold. They were then doused with delousing powder and given uniforms. Little consideration was given to sizing of these uniforms, and the shirts and trousers issued were often too big or too small. No underwear was provided. Uniforms usually had blue and white vertical stripes, but as populations grew in concentration camps, shortages of standard issue striped uniforms led to the SS improvising by using clothing stolen from those deported painted with distinctive markings on the back instead. Forcing new arrivals at concentration camps to wear uniforms was part of the effort to dehumanise them. The stripes on the clothing were supposed to make prisoners instantly recognisable, particularly when they were working outside the camp.

Men and women were separated and forced to live in cramped, vermin-infested barracks – many of which had been originally designed as horse sheds. They worked for 12 hours a day in all weather conditions with very little food. At night they slept on straw in rows of wooden bunks that had several people crammed into each berth. Lice were everywhere. When prisoners died in their sleep, those in their barrack had to carry their corpses out for the morning roll call to ensure that the register of prisoner numbers tallied.

In the KL

Life in concentration camps was a relentless assault on the physical and mental strength of prisoners. Their chances of survival were slim and they had to endure ongoing Nazi attempts to break their will.

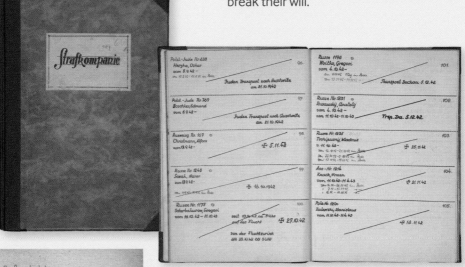

Top: In many concentration camps, prisoners judged to have broken rules were sent to the *Strafkompanie* (punishment company). Prisoners in these companies were forced to do the hardest labour on reduced rations. This punishment company register is from Natzweiler in occupied France. Many of the prisoners listed did not survive. The SS drew a line through the names of those who died.

Top left: Almost 21,000 Roma lived in the 'Gypsy family camp' in Auschwitz-Birkenau. This was a fenced-off area where Roma families were kept together. Despite brave physical resistance from its inhabitants, the family camp was liquidated by the SS on 2 August 1944. Fifteen-year-old Austrian Roma Johann Stojka and his brother Karl were sent from Auschwitz-Birkenau to Buchenwald. The rest of their family were sent to other camps. During his time in Buchenwald Johann risked his life by writing a book of poems with accompanying drawings. They describe his ongoing hunger and maltreatment during his time in Buchenwald.

Left: Eva Hamburger spent her 21st birthday as a slave labourer in Barth, a sub-camp of Ravensbrück. Her friend Klara Rakos carved this mini cello in secret as a present for her. Before the war Eva had aspired to be a professional cellist in Budapest, like her mother. For some prisoners, survival relied on support networks and trying to retain the memory of life outside the camp.

Bottom left: Daily prisoner rations usually consisted of thin soup, tasteless 'coffee' and a small piece of bread. This bread was often made using sawdust. Prisoners collected their rations in bowls like this. If a prisoner's bowl was lost or stolen, they received no food. Distribution of food was supervised by prisoners called *Blockälteste* (block elders).

A lack of adequate washing facilities led to conditions such as diarrhoea, typhus and dysentery becoming rife – and virtually non-existent medical care meant these were often fatal. Hundreds of prisoners died daily through illness, malnutrition and exhaustion, and many others were murdered at the hands of the SS through beatings and summary executions. Some prisoners were able to establish support networks with people within the same prisoner category or from the same country, but the system was designed to break their will and ensure their total compliance. Day-to-day survival depended on a range of factors, but ultimately relied on luck.

Taken for Biological Experiments

SS doctors subjected concentration camp prisoners to inhumane medical experiments. Some of these experiments were intended to find ways to help the German military, while others were based on speculative race theories that the Nazis wanted to try and prove. Nazi doctors saw prisoners as expendable and were unconcerned whether they died as a direct result of the experiments – indeed, in some cases, prisoners used in experiments were executed so that post-mortem tests could be performed on their bodies. Those who survived were often left permanently disabled.

In Dachau Dr Sigmund Rascher performed experiments for the *Luftwaffe* (German Air Force), using prisoners to investigate

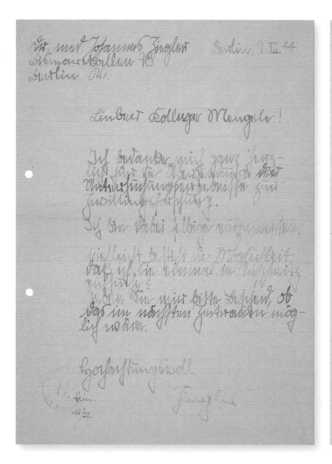

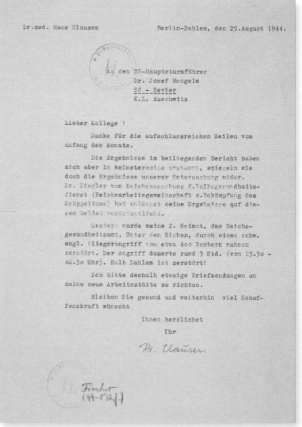

Opposite: SS doctor Josef Mengele particularly valued experimenting on twins. These letters from elite research institutions thanked Mengele for sharing his 'research' in this area. Mengele's work killed hundreds of twins in Auschwitz.

the effects of altitude and hypothermia on the body. His data helped the *Luftwaffe* plan for long-range missions and bail out procedures. In Ravensbrück, medical staff looking for ways of treating diseases affecting German soldiers in combat – including typhoid, yellow fever and malaria – tested anti-bacterial drugs on female prisoners. Secretly taken photographs show prisoners whose legs have been deliberately wounded and infected with bacteria, dirt and shards of glass.

Maintaining control

The SS used violence and the threat of violence to maintain control of the concentration camps. By giving some prisoners responsibilities over others in return for privileges, they created hierarchies between prisoners that restricted opportunities for organised resistance. *Kapos* were the main set of prisoners chosen by the SS to supervise other prisoners and were often the major enforcers of discipline in the camp. Some were Jewish, but most were selected from those who had been incarcerated as career criminals. *Kapos* were marked out with an armband and issued with a wooden baton. Although they received preferential treatment for performing their roles, they faced punishment if they did not maintain control and use batons to beat their fellow inmates. Some *Kapos* tried to use their positions to mitigate the conditions of those around them, but others were brutally cruel. Prisoners often hated *Kapos* more than the SS.

When the SS did intervene directly, they were ruthless – so were the women and soldiers drafted in to assist them. Their

Herta Lutz

Until 1943, Herta Lutz had only ever worked in factories, but at the age of 21 she was one of eight young women from her workplace chosen to become an *Aufseherin* (female guard) in the concentration camps. She embraced her training at Ravensbrück concentration camp and within a matter of weeks became a feared guard at Grüneberg sub-camp. With her loyal dog, Greif, she enjoyed her work. She was renowned for encouraging the dog to urinate on prisoners.

Hala Lichtenstein	Hala Lichtenstein was deported to Auschwitz-Birkenau in 1943, at the age of 22. She managed to get work in the camp's storage warehouses sorting victims' belongings. This was a highly sought-after position among prisoners.
Anita Lasker	Anita Lasker was sent to Auschwitz-Birkenau at the age of 18. She was a talented cellist and was recruited into the women's orchestra at the camp. She was forced to play upbeat marches as prisoners walked in procession to and from work. She also had to perform for the SS.

use of punishment to impose discipline was supposed to be regulated, but in reality was unpredictable, indiscriminate and often lethal. Male guards were armed with guns and whips, which they used to intimidate inmates and enforce discipline. Male and female guards also used their heavy, military boots as weapons, kicking and stamping on unarmed and emaciated prisoners, sometimes causing fatal injuries. Prisoners were powerless against SS violence.

Left: The number of prisoners in concentration camps grew after the outbreak of war, creating a demand for more SS guards. Otto Hörgelow joined the SS in 1937, but was not sent to work at a concentration camp until 1940. At 45 years old he was too old to fight, but served in various camps between 1940 and 1945.

Opposite, clockwise from top left: Hala Lichtenstein's work in the camp's storage warehouses allowed her to secure extra food and clothing from the packed suitcases. One day the SS ordered that workers wear a black apron. Hala managed to find this one in a pile of clothes. She also helped the underground resistance movement by smuggling gold to them; Concentration camp dress used by Claudette Bloch to talk about her experiences in Auschwitz; Anita Lasker's role in the orchestra at Auschwitz-Birkenau meant that she was given extra bread. She exchanged some of this bread for this red, woollen jumper. She wore it day and night to protect herself against the harsh winter.

Claudette Bloch

Biologist Claudette Bloch was among the first group of French women to arrive in Auschwitz in June 1942. She was 32. Most of the transport were sent to the gas chambers, but Claudette was selected for labour. She was given the number 7963. Claudette almost died from malnutrition, but managed to survive when she was sent to work as a research scientist in Rajsko, a sub-camp of Auschwitz. She was forced to assist with work to create synthetic rubber using dandelion plants.

CHAPTER TEN

Breakdown

B y the start of 1944, Germany's war effort was becoming increasingly stretched. The German military was being driven back on the Eastern Front and was preparing to defend against a major Allied invasion from the west. Its losses were becoming overwhelming and their attempts to find additional workers and weaponry were growing desperate. In March, Germany turned on its ally Hungary and invaded. Hitler made this decision when he discovered that Hungary, having become convinced about the inevitability of a German defeat, had been trying to seek a way out of the war. Outraged, he issued orders for his forces to occupy the country on 19 March. Hungary's government had a history of discriminating against its Jewish population, but with few exceptions had largely refused Nazi demands to deport its 500,000 Jews. With the German invasion these restrictions no longer existed, and Europe's largest remaining Jewish population now came under Nazi control.

On 6 June 1944, D-Day, the western Allies launched their long-awaited invasion of western Europe. As Allied forces advanced on Germany from both west and east, they began to discover first-hand evidence of the Nazis' programme of annihilation. The Nazis hurriedly increased efforts to conceal the traces of their crimes. As concentration camps came within range of Allied forces, they began a series of mass evacuations, known as 'death marches'. These death marches would ultimately represent the final throes of the concentration camp network, but would bring more suffering for those forced to embark on them.

Opposite: The Nazis wanted to eradicate Jewish culture across Europe. They destroyed Jewish cemeteries and used the headstones for building materials and road surfaces. This gravestone was repurposed as a millstone. The remaining original Hebrew text reads, 'For these I cry; my eyes, my eyes are shedding tears'.

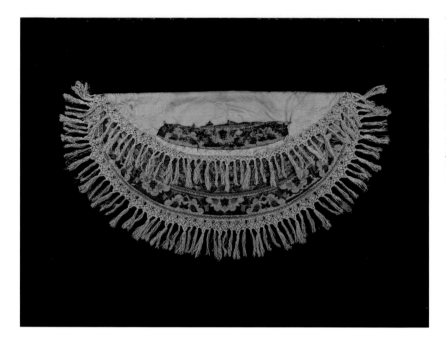

Occupation and Collaboration

Under Nazi pressure the Hungarians established a pro-German antisemitic government. The moderate prime minister Miklós Kállay was removed and the rabid antisemite Döme Sztójay was installed in his place. Willing collaborators were appointed to key positions of power. The Hungarian Army, police and civil administration were put at the disposal of the *Gestapo* and the SS. The head of the office for Jewish affairs, Adolf Eichmann, took up residence in a commandeered house in Budapest. Under his leadership, the German authorities and their Hungarian collaborators began to deport Jews at a ferocious pace. Young men and women were taken as slave labourers to support Germany's deteriorating war effort, while the rest were taken to their deaths.

From mid-May to mid-July 1944, more than 440,000 Hungarian Jews were sent to Auschwitz-Birkenau. An extension to the railway spur was completed to bring trains carrying victims through the main gate and directly into the camp, in order to make the murder process more efficient. Trains were emptied directly on a new purpose-built ramp and selections were made within sight of the gas chamber buildings. Those not immediately designated for death were held for murderous slave labour. As Auschwitz-Birkenau entered its deadliest phase, the gas chambers became overwhelmed by the vast numbers of people being killed there and the process became increasingly chaotic.

Hiding the Traces

The Nazis went to great efforts to conceal their killing programme. In June 1942, SS officer Paul Blobel had been instructed by Reinhard Heydrich to initiate *Aktion 1005*, a project to remove the traces of the Nazis' campaign of mass murder in central and eastern Europe. Under Blobel's command, Jewish concentration camp prisoners were forced to disinter mass graves of Jewish victims and burn the bodies on huge pyres. The decision to embark on the *Aktion* had been driven by information that the Allies had growing knowledge of the Nazis' programme of annihilation. The pace and scale of these efforts grew as it became clearer to the Nazis that their territory in eastern Europe was under increasing threat from the Soviet advance.

As the Allies drew closer, the Nazis began to dismantle camps and burn millions of documents. The death camps at Belzec, Sobibor and Treblinka had been dismantled between 1943 and 1944 and all visible traces had been removed. In the case of the latter two, the decision to close these camps had been accelerated by prisoner uprisings, and in all three places by the time the Soviet Army arrived there was little immediate evidence of what had occurred there. Despite these efforts, it was impossible for the Nazis to remove all traces of their crimes.

Alongside their efforts to remove the physical traces of annihilation, the Nazis embarked on a sustained propaganda campaign to mask and obscure the reality of what they were doing. In 1944, they allowed an International Red Cross delegation to visit the Theresienstadt ghetto, just outside Prague. The ghetto had long been used by the Nazis to deceive the world about their programme of annihilation and to suggest that their treatment of Europe's Jews was benign in both intent and implementation. A propaganda film was made there in 1944

Rescue in Hungary

The Nazis began the process of deportation from the outer regions of Hungary, moving towards the capital, Budapest. The fast pace of this meant that for many help did not arrive in time. But in Budapest, where the only surviving Jewish community remained, individuals and international agencies were moved to intervene before deportations from the city began. Foreign diplomats and representatives of humanitarian organisations used their status and influence to try and help Hungarian Jews. They issued protective documents and set up safe houses in the so-called international ghetto in the city. Jews with certificates of protection supplied by neutral countries were mostly contained in this area. The passes did not guarantee survival — and were not always respected — but they saved a large number of lives.

In June 1944 pressure began to grow on Hungarian regent Miklós Horthy to order an end to deportations. On 7 July, a month after the Allied landings in northern Europe, he did so. In October 1944, a German-backed coup brought the fascist Arrow Cross Party to power in Hungary, placing the Jews who remained in Budapest back in mortal danger. The new regime carried out a frenzied campaign of terror against the city's Jewish population. They massacred thousands and resumed deportations. Against this backdrop international rescue efforts grew. As the Soviet Army closed in on Budapest during the fascist regime's final chaotic months, Arrow Cross murder squads intensified their activities. Jewish men, women and children were pulled at random from the ghetto and executed in the street or shot along the banks of the River Danube. Their bodies fell into the water below.

Swedish diplomat Raoul Wallenberg arrived in Budapest in mid-1944 to try and save as many Jews as possible. Members of his staff used this typewriter to create thousands of *Schutzpässe* (protective passes). As Sweden was a neutral country, it was technically able to provide this protection to people.

Right: These photographs are from an album compiled by Karl Höcker, adjutant to the commandant of Auschwitz. They were taken during the camp's most lethal months, in summer 1944. They show official visits to the camp, as well as SS guards at leisure in Solahütte – a retreat near Auschwitz used to reward those who had performed their duties well.

following the International Red Cross visit, which was to be used to bolster these claims. Thousands of people were deported to death camps in advance of filming, in order to avoid the ghetto appearing overcrowded.

Forced Evacuations

In the winter of 1944–1945, the Nazis began to evacuate prisoners from camps near the advancing Soviet front line back towards the Reich. They wanted to force these prisoners to work in support of the collapsing German war effort and prevent them from falling into enemy hands. The majority of the evacuations – known as 'death marches' – were conducted on foot, but trains and other forms of transport were occasionally used. Those who were considered unable to make the journey were either killed or left to die. Many who set out on the marches had survived years in ghettos and camps.

These photographs, taken by camp officials in the summer of 1944, document the selection of Hungarian Jews at Auschwitz-Birkenau. They capture the chaos of arrival, the moment of selection and the false calm of the final moments before people entered the gas chambers. They are the only known photographic evidence of this process.

Above: Jews arriving at Auschwitz-Birkenau in the summer of 1944 were taken directly into the camp on a newly built ramp. They were forced to disembark from the trains and sorted into columns. Nazi personnel stood at the front of these columns and decided who should be killed immediately and who should be worked to death as slave labourers. Babies and their mothers were always murdered. This woman, and the child in her arms, have just been selected for the nearby gas chambers.

Above: The journey from the selections ramp to the gas chambers took people through the centre of Auschwitz-Birkenau. The girl on the left of this photo is looking towards the prisoner barracks that lined the path.

Above: In summer 1944 the gas chambers at Auschwitz-Birkenau were operating beyond their capacity. This led to frequent delays. People selected for murder were told that they were heading for showers and were forced to wait in a small grove outside the gas chamber building. Mothers took the opportunity to give their children some of the food they had packed for the journey. As the small child handing a flower to a friend or sibling suggests, many of those waiting were oblivious to what was really happening.

Above: People selected for slave labour at Auschwitz-Birkenau were sent to be showered and disinfected, Their heads were shaved and they were given identifying tattoos on their forearms. This photograph was taken shortly after the completion of this process and the tattoo is visible on the forearm of the woman in the front.

Meine Lieben, ich bin hier mit meinem Mann,
Schwester u. Neffen, sind alle gesund u. geht es uns gut.
Mein Mann erhielt gestern ein Paket von unserer Haus-
frau u. bitte ich Dich, es ihr zu bestätigen. Sage auch
Gerty unseren innigsten Dank. Sie soll Boža Šmíd von
uns grüssen. Ich hoffe euch alle gesund u. zufrieden.
Deine Altern waren bei unserer Abreise vollkommen ge-
sund, auch meine u. von Gerty.
   Lasst bald von euch hören. Peter sieht gut
aus u. freut sich auf Nachrichten von euch.
   Viele Grüsse u. Küsse Qüere
                                        Zdena Isidor.

20. X. 1943.

Left: The SS forced some new arrivals at Auschwitz-Birkenau to send deceptive postcards back home. This was intended to trick victims' loved ones into believing the sender was alive and well in order to make further deportations from the same area easier. Those who wrote the postcards were usually killed before they were sent. Zdena Isidor wrote this postcard to her cousin Olga in Prague on arrival at Auschwitz-Birkenau. Instead of Olga's first name, Zdena used 'Lechem', the Hebrew word for bread. This coded message indicated she was starving. Zdena was sent to the gas chambers shortly after writing the postcard.

Opposite left: Freddie Knoller took this badge from a communist prisoner who died during a death march. Freddie believed his chances of survival would be higher if he was identified as a political prisoner rather than a Jew. As the Allies drew closer, Nazi guards murdered prisoners at an increasing rate and Jews were most in danger.

Opposite right: As the Soviet Army advanced towards Auschwitz-Birkenau, SS guards were instructed to destroy the remaining crematoria. Most of these buildings – which contained the gas chambers – were blown up in January 1945. Despite these efforts, the structure and remnants of the buildings were clearly visible. This fragment was part of an oven frame in the crematoria.

Tens of thousands of people died of starvation, disease and exhaustion from walking vast distances in the bitter winter cold. Those who could not keep up were shot on the spot, their bodies usually remaining where they fell. The marches led prisoners from the edges of German-occupied territory right into

the heart of the collapsing Reich. Columns of prisoners trudged through streets and roads in Germany and Austria revealing first-hand evidence to those who witnessed them exactly what had been done in the name of the so-called thousand-year Reich. Some people were appalled at the sight of the human suffering, but others saw it as proof of the impoverished and disease-ridden Jews that they had been taught to despise. Up to one-third of the 714,000 prisoners who embarked on the death marches did not survive.

Falling Apart

The death marches eventually reached the few remaining concentration camps in Germany, leading to terrible overcrowding. Accommodation blocks within these camps were already well beyond capacity and were completely unable to cope with the thousands of additional people. Barracks overflowed and food supplies became almost non-existent. In some camps, tents were used to house the overflow of prisoners. As disease and starvation raged, death rates rose and systems of order began to completely collapse. In some camps, commandants created fenced-off areas called 'death zones' where selected prisoners were deliberately starved and left to die.

At Buchenwald the so-called 'Little Camp', which was positioned at the bottom end of the site and separated from the remainder of the accommodation blocks, was designated as a 'death zone'. Despite the appalling conditions, a group of adult male prisoners incarcerated there worked with the communist resistance to make Barrack 66 a 'children's block'. They moved all male prisoners under 16 – who were mostly Jews – into this barrack and tried to shelter them from disease. The *Blockälteste* (block elder) Antonin Kalina, a Czech communist, worked to protect the 900 boys as the SS turned on the remaining Jews in the camp.

Above: Gisele Friedman was one of 10,000 prisoners sent on a death march from Auschwitz. She spent five days travelling in a covered train followed by five days walking in freezing conditions. After another five days in an open truck she arrived at Bergen-Belsen. She wore these shoes and carried this flask throughout her journey.

Opposite: These photographs were taken in secret from inside the doorway of Crematoria V by Alberto Errera, a member of the *Sonderkommando* at Auschwitz-Birkenau. They were intended to provide evidence of the murders at the camp. They show bodies being burned in the open because the crematoria could not cope with the numbers being killed. Up to 12,000 people were murdered each day during this period.

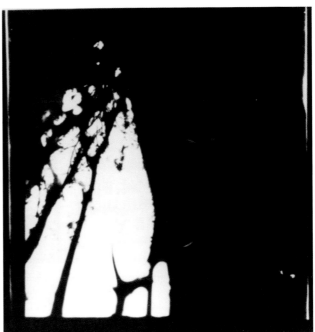

Right: Jan Hartmann drew this picture shortly after surviving a death march from Czechowice to Bielsko in January 1945. Those lying by the roadside have either died from exhaustion or been shot by the SS for being unable to keep up.

CHAPTER ELEVEN

Afterwards

B y the end of the war, Allied soldiers had liberated hundreds of thousands of prisoners from concentration camps. They freed others from death marches and improvised sites of incarceration. These liberations were not a strategic aim for Allied troops, but became a general part of the Allied advance. Among those they found in the remaining camps were Jewish and Roma survivors of the Nazis' programme of annihilation. Most were starving, sick and exhausted. Some felt joy and relief at finally being freed, others were consumed with grief and guilt. Many were too weak to understand what was happening.

Allied soldiers categorised liberated prisoners as Displaced Persons (DPs) and housed them in DP camps. Initially these camps were grouped by nationality, until mounting pressure from Jewish groups eventually led to Jews being generally placed together, in recognition of the specific nature of what they had experienced and the challenges they faced.

The men, women and children now released from Nazi terror faced futures shaped by its impact. They had to recuperate physically, find new homes and start new lives. Some would never fully recover from the injuries they had received. Many had lost everyone they knew. After years of suffering, they faced a difficult recovery and an uncertain future.

Liberation Comes

The Soviets reached Majdanek in July 1944; this was the first concentration camp to be liberated. As the war drew to a close, advancing Allied soldiers discovered many more. The

camps they encountered on the edges of the Nazis' shrinking
territory were usually empty and abandoned. But those they
found as they entered what remained of the Reich were full.
What they came across in Dachau, Buchenwald, Mauthausen,
Bergen-Belsen and elsewhere was unlike anything they had
encountered before. Battle-hardened troops wept at the sights
that confronted them. The scenes they witnessed were seen in
newsreels across the world.

After the End

For some prisoners, liberation came just in time – for others
it was too late. Soldiers were shocked by the emaciated

Opposite: Diseases such as typhus, tuberculosis and dysentery continued to claim lives after liberation. This photograph shows severely ill survivors being washed and deloused in the 'human laundry' in Belsen. This helped to prevent the spread of disease. To the disgust of some survivors, a lack of Allied resources meant it was partially staffed by German nurses and doctors.

Right: This photograph shows women in Belsen choosing clean clothes from the clothing supply store. This store became known by the nickname 'Harrods'. Clothes were donated by relief organisations or taken from nearby towns. Women were also offered lipstick. After years of living in rags this process played a big role in helping survivors to feel human again.

people, describing them as 'living skeletons'. They handed out chocolate and other food from their emergency ration packs, desperate to try and help. The effects of starvation meant that survivors could not tolerate rich food, however, and sometimes these acts of intended kindness resulted in illness or even death. Allied armies more broadly were unprepared and under-resourced for the humanitarian catastrophe they faced, and relied on the help of relief organisations and volunteers to tackle the crisis.

Medical teams in Belsen tried to manage starvation with a special food mixture used during the 1943 Bengal famine. They also introduced intravenous feeding for those too weak to feed themselves. Many survivors became hysterical upon

Then comes the english doktor wit the
Swith-sister.

Opposite top: This booklet was drawn by 14-year-old Eva Sachselová for Andrew Matthews. Matthews was one of 96 British medical students sent to Belsen to help survivors in May 1945. The booklet was to thank him for his kindness and friendship in helping Eva and her sister Hana to recover in the makeshift hospital.

Opposite bottom: Jewish children with no surviving family were sent to children's homes in France, Switzerland and Britain. Britain was persuaded to accept up to 1,000 Jewish orphans, but in the end was only able to find 732. This photograph shows them in Prague before their flight to Britain. The group became known as 'The Boys' – even though there were 80 girls among them.

seeing intravenous feeding kits, associating them with methods and equipment that the SS used for medical experimentation and murder.

Of the 90,000 Jewish prisoners liberated at Belsen, at least 20,000 died within weeks. Eventually the situation begun to stabilise. Survivors slowly began to recover their strength and adjust to their new reality.

Building New Worlds

Many Jews felt there was no future for them in Europe after everything they had experienced. The USA and Palestine became the two most sought-after destinations for them to start new lives, but Britain still controlled Palestine and made emigration there almost impossible. Jews caught trying to enter the territory without permission were sent to internment camps in Cyprus. Some countries were willing to take orphaned Jewish children, but were reluctant to accept large numbers of adults. DPs were left feeling stranded, ignored and unwanted.

In addition to the lack of opportunities afforded to Jewish DPs after the war, active anti-Jewish hostility also continued. In some places Jews were killed by people who had taken their houses when they returned to reclaim them; in others they struggled to get back the things that had been taken from them. In July 1946 a pogrom erupted in Kielce, Poland. Local mobs converged on a Jewish committee building after a non-Jewish Polish boy claimed he had been hidden in it after being kidnapped (something he later admitted he had made up). In the violence that followed 42 Jewish people were killed.

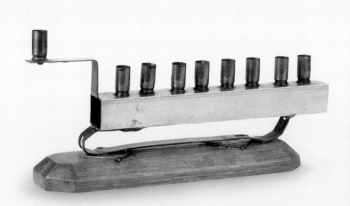

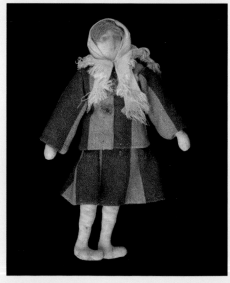

Surviving Survival

In the chaos of post-war Europe over 250,000 Jewish people needed to either return home or find a new one. Although many were former concentration camp prisoners liberated from Nazi Europe, most were people who had escaped to the Soviet Union earlier in the war and were now returning. They were temporarily housed in Displaced Persons (DP) camps or refugee centres run by the military and the United Nations. DP camps became places where people gradually re-established social, cultural and religious identities. Some people lived in them for many years.

DPs were offered classes in activities such as doll-making and painting to help deal with their experiences. This process encouraged survivors to recover both mental strength and physical dexterity. At Belsen a group formed an Occupational Therapy Department and set up a three-day exhibition of items created by fellow DPs. Most child survivors had lost years of education as well as their childhoods. Even older children were often unable to read or write. *Yeshivas* (religious schools) were also established.

Opposite top: A makeshift school in Belsen DP camp.

Left: Gena Goldfinger wore this dress at her wedding to British soldier Norman Turgel. The couple married within months of meeting at Belsen. Many young survivors were eager to start new families. Allowances were made by some rabbis so that people whose husbands or wives had disappeared could remarry. DP camps soon had the highest birth rates in post-war Europe.

Opposite far left: This *hanukkiah*, a candelabrum used for *Hanukkah*, was made from parts of a Sten gun by a soldier in the British Army's Jewish Brigade. He did this to help 83 Jewish children celebrate the first *Hanukkah* in Belsen after liberation. *Hanukkah* is a Jewish festival of light and had a particularly powerful resonance in 1945.

Opposite left: A doll made by a former prisoner in Belsen during occupational therapy sessions.

Right: The soldiers who liberated the camps knew they needed to create a permanent record of what they were witnessing. This sketch of Belsen was drawn by war artist Bryan de Grineau. De Grineau was working for the British newspaper, *The Illustrated London News.* The handwritten notes in the margin evidence his struggle to describe what he saw.

LARGE
TENT FILLED WITH
RECUMBENT FORMS
ANY LIVING TOO
WEAK TO MOVE.

CHILD
WITH
TIN OF
WATER

Bryan de Grineau — 1945
BELSEN CONCENTRATION CAMP GERMANY

19¼ x 11½

Responsibility and Judgement

A s the war in Europe came to an end, the Allies intensified their efforts to shape the peace. In 1943 a joint declaration signed by the US, Britain and the Soviet Union during a conference in Moscow had committed the countries to investigating and putting on trial perpetrators of Nazi atrocities. This agreement formed the basis of the post-war prosecution process. The legal proceedings that it led to ultimately established the foundations of international criminal justice.

The Allies used both new and existing tools of justice to prosecute Nazi war criminals. In 1945, they established an international court in Nuremberg, Germany, to put on trial some of the regime's most senior surviving members. The transnational nature of this trial was intended to reflect the international character of the crimes of the individuals who would be taking the stand and acknowledge the fact that it was beyond the remit of any single nation to assume responsibility for prosecuting them. After much discussion, 24 German military and political leaders were selected for trial – each was intended to represent a different part of Hitler's administration. Lawyers from the Britain, the US, France and the Soviet Union worked together to reconcile their own legal systems into a new process of justice. This became the International Military Tribunal (IMT) in Nuremberg and was the first international criminal court.

Diese Schandtaten: Eure Schuld!

Evidence used in the IMT mostly came from captured Nazi documents. These represented a comprehensive record of Nazi crimes, which Allied lawyers believed were more reliable than eyewitnesses who they thought were too psychologically damaged to testify reliably and were liable to collapse under cross-examination. Huge piles of documents were collected for each charge against every defendant.

Alongside the IMT, individual countries also pursued Nazis and their collaborators in a large number of smaller national trials in the years immediately after the war. In parallel with this, the victorious Allies oversaw a series of 'denazification' programmes aimed at the whole of German society. The intention of these activities was to force Germans to confront what had been done in their name, to exclude former Nazis from professional sectors such as the civil service and to remove all remaining traces of Nazism from society. The policy was inconsistently applied and its success was mixed, allowing many perpetrators to return to pre-war roles and positions of status and responsibility.

By the end of the 1940s, co-operation between the victorious nations in Europe had ended. Relationships between the

Josef Kramer

Josef Kramer, commandant of Belsen, was arrested during the camp's liberation in April 1945. He had worked in concentration camps for 11 years and had previously been responsible for running the gas chambers at Auschwitz-Birkenau. He was notorious among prisoners for his cruelty. During the trial, survivors reported that conditions in Belsen worsened after Kramer took command. Dubbed the 'Beast of Belsen' by the British press, he was convicted of his crimes and hanged in December 1945.

Irma Grese

Irma Grese was one of 16 women tried at the Belsen camp trials. She was 22 years old. Grese had been a guard at Auschwitz-Birkenau before transferring to Belsen. She was described by witnesses as the worst female camp guard. Former prisoners explained how they feared her beating them with her homemade whip. The press labelled her 'the Bitch of Belsen.' Grese's lawyer tried to excuse her actions because of her age, but she was found guilty and hanged in December 1945.

Hermann Göring

Hermann Göring was the most senior Nazi on trial in Nuremberg. He spent 12 days in the dock defending Hitler's war policy. He claimed that he knew nothing about plans to exterminate Europe's Jews. However, evidence presented during the trial proved he was at meetings where these plans were discussed. Göring was sentenced to death, but swallowed a hidden cyanide capsule in his cell and died just two hours before he was due to be hanged.

Carmen Mory

Carmen Mory was tried in 1947 for her conduct as a *Kapo* at Ravensbrück concentration camp. Several fellow prisoners accused her of torturing sick inmates and beating others to death. Mory protested that, as a prisoner herself, she was forced to do this to survive. These claims were dismissed by the judges. Wearing her signature dark fur coat, Mory swayed and crossed herself as she was sentenced to death by hanging. She killed herself in her cell before the death sentence could be carried out.

Hans Eisele

Dr Hans Eisele was described as the 'Butcher of Buchenwald'. He was accused of administering lethal injections to prisoners sick with tuberculosis and conducting experimental surgery on others. US judges sentenced him to death at the Dachau trials in 1945. Eisele appealed the sentence, claiming that the evidence was untrustworthy. His sentence was changed to imprisonment. Two years later he was sentenced to death again for murdering hundreds of prisoners at Buchenwald. Again, his death sentence was commuted to a prison sentence. The length of this sentence was later reduced and he was released in 1952. He resumed his medical career, but fled to Egypt when further allegations about him emerged. He lived there under a false name for the rest of his life.

Albert Speer

Albert Speer, Hitler's minister of armaments, was among the defendants at the IMT in Nuremberg. He was responsible for the exploitation of millions of slave labourers from concentration camps. During the trial he openly condemned Hitler's regime and denied all knowledge of the mass murder of Europe's Jews. As a result, he developed a reputation as the 'decent Nazi'. Despite his seniority, and his close friendship with Hitler, he was not sentenced to death but 20 years in prison instead. In his later years Speer acknowledged that the account he provided at the IMT was incomplete and that he was more aware of the Nazis' policies of annihilation than he had claimed.

Soviet Union and the other Allies had deteriorated into a new international conflict. This would soon become known as the Cold War.

Evading Justice

In the final weeks of the war, those responsible for mass murder looked for ways to escape justice. Adolf Hitler and Joseph Goebbels were among hundreds who killed themselves rather than risk capture. Heinrich Himmler, Hermann Göring, Odilo Globočnik and many lower ranking Nazis took their lives while in Allied custody. Other Nazi war criminals went into hiding or attempted to flee to countries where they would

Top: These sketches of the Nuremberg trial were drawn by David Low, a cartoonist from New Zealand. Low attended the trial as an official war artist. Spectators and journalists were fascinated by the sight of the defendants in the courtroom. Many were disappointed at how ordinary the notorious figures looked. Low attempted to capture this unexpected normality.

Right: Anita Lasker, a Jewish survivor of Auschwitz-Birkenau and Belsen, appeared as a witness at the Belsen camp trial. She used this pass to enter the court. Anita was unhappy about the way her testimony was received, feeling that the court did not believe her because she could not recall certain times or dates.

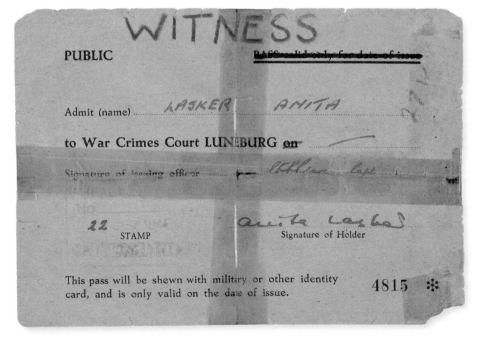

Unlike the IMT, the British military relied heavily on witness testimony during the Ravensbrück trials in 1947. The prosecution used 36 drawings by former French political prisoner Violette Lecoq as evidence of conditions in the predominantly female camp. All the witnesses were women, as were 21 of the 38 perpetrators on trial.

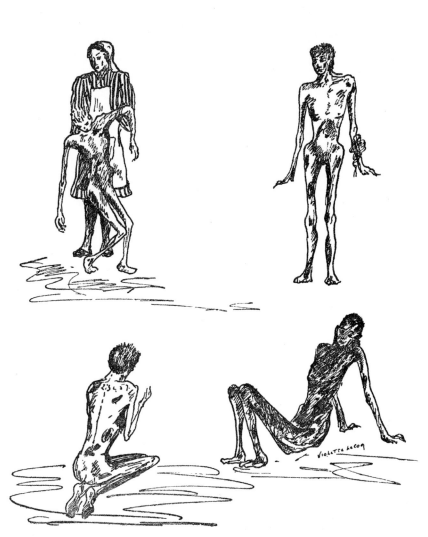

23. — *Les âmes n'y sont plus...*

20. — *Hygiène...*

34. — *Champ d'honneur...*

Hadassah (Ada) Bimko

Hadassah (Ada) Bimko was a Polish Jewish doctor who had survived two years in Auschwitz-Birkenau and Bergen-Belsen. After liberation she was central to medical relief efforts at Belsen. As a witness at the Belsen trials, she confronted those who had murdered her parents, brother, husband and six-year-old son. Her testimony helped to ensure that several perpetrators were convicted. Her accounts of the selections at Auschwitz-Birkenau were seized upon by the media. This was one of the first eyewitness accounts of this process read by the British public.

Hersch Lauterpacht

Hersch Lauterpacht was a scholar of law whose studies took him from Lwów and Vienna to the London School of Economics, then to a professorship at the University of Cambridge. During the war he proposed new international laws to protect individuals from the crimes of governments. These became the basis for modern human rights laws. As a member of the British delegation at Nuremberg, he discovered that his entire family in Lwów had been murdered, apart from his niece Inka.

be beyond the reach of all relevant authorities. Although some of these men were eventually captured, many lived out the rest of their lives in freedom.

Hitler died by suicide as the Soviet Army closed in on his bunker in Berlin. Before doing so he dictated his last political will and testament to his secretary, Traudl Junge. In the final words he ever committed to paper, he implored the German people to continue 'with merciless resistance against the universal poisoners of all people, international Jewry'.

Crimes Without a Name

In 1945, existing international laws were considered inadequate for charging the perpetrators at Nuremberg. Two Polish Jewish lawyers argued for the inclusion of two new international crimes. Hersch Lauterpacht proposed 'crimes against humanity', focusing on offences committed against individuals while Rafael Lemkin lobbied for the charge of 'genocide', which addressed crimes committed against groups. Lemkin invented

Opposite: These photographs show civilians forced to visit nearby concentration camps and watch films documenting the atrocities committed there. The Allies did this to shame the German population, especially those who claimed ignorance of the regime's crimes. By the end of the 1940s British and American attitudes towards Germany had begun to change, as former enemies became allies in the developing Cold War.

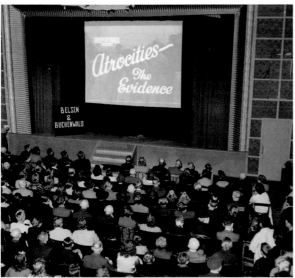

The Trial of Adolf Eichmann

The 1961–1962 trial of Adolf Eichmann in Jerusalem was followed across the world, and brought a renewed focus on questions of post-war justice. A series of trials in Germany through the 1960s led to the removal of several war criminals from their jobs and became part of the ongoing process of the country confronting its past. Although the number of trials dwindled, the prosecution of war criminals continued into the twenty-first century. In the end, although most high-ranking Nazis were sentenced to death or imprisonment, many lower level perpetrators faced neither prosecution nor punishment.

Adolf Eichmann giving evidence at his trial in Jerusalem.

the word 'genocide' by combining the words *genos* (Greek for 'race' or 'family') and *cide* (from the Latin for 'kill'). Lemkin's ideas were prompted by the mass murder of Armenians by the Ottoman Turks during the First World War. The two concepts were first used in the Nuremberg proceedings. Today they are central to international law. The Convention on the Prevention and Punishment of the Crime of Genocide was adopted by the United Nations General Assembly on 9 December 1948. It was the first modern human rights treaty. It was not until the 1990s that this convention was applied, when two international criminal tribunals were created to address atrocities in the former Yugoslavia and Rwanda.

Abraham Sutzkever

Abraham Sutzkever was among the few surviving Jews from Vilnius, Lithuania. He was called to testify at Nuremberg as one of only three Jewish witnesses. Although he was a well-established Yiddish poet, he struggled to find words to describe the atrocities committed against Vilnius's Jews. He insisted on remaining standing as he recalled his baby son's murder in the Vilna ghetto. He delivered the testimony as if saying the *Kaddish*, the Jewish prayer for the dead.

Ernst Mettbach

Ernst Mettbach was a Roma survivor of several concentration camps. He was a witness at the doctors' trial in Nuremberg. His testimony formed part of the case against Dr Wilhelm Beiglböck. Beiglböck conducted sea water experiments on Roma prisoners at Dachau. Ernst told the court he was ruled out of these tests by a fever, but smuggled clean drinking water to a relative participating in the trials. While on the stand he revealed that his father and five brothers and sisters were all killed at Auschwitz-Birkenau.

Samuel Rajzman

Samuel Rajzman was a former member of the *Sonderkommando* at the Treblinka death camp. He gave evidence at Nuremberg as one of Treblinka's few Jewish survivors. He told the court that, while working in the gas chamber building, he witnessed thousands of people being murdered daily. He recalled how his friend found a photograph of Samuel's wife and child when they were sorting through the clothing of murdered Jews. This was the only thing he had left to remember them by.

Rafael Lemkin

Rafael Lemkin, a lawyer in Warsaw, fled Poland after the Nazi invasion in September 1939, reaching the US in 1941. He invented the legal concept of 'genocide', believing that international law should prohibit the 'intent to destroy' ethnic, national, racial and religious groups. As an adviser to the US Chief Prosecutor, he campaigned to have his new legal concept introduced at Nuremberg. During the trial he learned that the Nazis had killed 49 members of his family, including his parents.

Arthur Greiser

Arthur Greiser was tried by a Polish court as the former governor of the Warthegau region of Nazi-occupied Poland. He was accused of causing the suffering and murder of thousands of Polish people – including Jews. Greiser claimed he was just following orders, but the trial found him personally responsible. He was found guilty of all charges, except one alleging that he personally committed murder or inflicted bodily harm. He was publicly hanged on 21 July 1946.

The Will for Revenge

In the immediate aftermath of liberation, newly released prisoners and the troops who freed them sometimes took immediate revenge on concentration camp personnel. This revenge took the form of beatings and even summary executions. In addition to these virtually instantaneous acts, some concentration camp guards who fled were tracked down and occasionally killed by Allied soldiers in the weeks that followed. Former Mauthausen Commandant Franz Ziereis was shot while trying to escape from Allied soldiers who had tracked him down in late May 1945. After being fatally wounded, he was interrogated by war crimes investigators. Once he was dead, his body was strung up on the fence of the Gusen sub-camp with the words 'Heil Hitler' and mocking swastikas and SS runes drawn on his naked back.

Across Europe, both governments and civilians struggled to reconcile the atrocities committed during the war with the demands of the new peace. In the months and years that followed the war, individuals and groups planned and organised revenge operations, targeting both war criminals and the German public at large.

Fate Unknown

In the years after the war, millions of people around the world still knew nothing about what had happened to their loved ones. They searched for any information in whatever ways they could. Several organisations, including the British Red Cross, assisted in these endeavours. In 1948 the efforts of these organisations were combined to form the International Tracing Service (ITS), which still exists today. The ITS developed into an archive containing over 30 million pages of documentation relating to the victims of Nazi persecution. It assists with attempts to find information about those who were lost. However, despite the efforts of the ITS and other archives like them, the scale of the Nazis' destruction means that for many people no traces will ever be found.

Wer KENNT und kann AUSKUNFT geben über

Gottlieb   seine Ehefrau Elsa, geb.   und deren Tochter Lily

Müller · Bilzing · Müller

Geb. am 1. Dezember 1888   Geb. am 8. Februar 1894   Geb. am 24. Februar 1922

Letzte Wiener Adresse: Wien, IX., Müllnergasse 33/10. Die Genannten wurden **1942 in Theresienstadt** interniert.

Um jegliche Nachricht bittet die Tochter:

Nurse Herta Müller

Epsom Country Hospital - Dorking Rd. **Epsom, Surrey** - England

Plakatdruck „Ehrenhof", IX., Berggasse 31

Above: Herta Müller put up this poster asking for information about her missing parents Gottlieb and Elsa and her sister Lily. Herta knew that they had been deported from Vienna to Theresienstadt in 1942, but had heard nothing else. She eventually found out that the Nazis murdered all three in Auschwitz-Birkenau.

Left: Marek Kellermann was a brush merchant from Bratislava, Czechoslovakia. In 1939 he deposited this tie pin in a branch of Barclays Bank while in London on business. He never returned to collect it. Nothing is known of what happened to Marek and all attempts to trace him have been unsuccessful. There are many like him.

After the war, Martin Meyer wrote letters to many organisations in search of his brother Arthur. Their responses confirmed that Arthur was deported from Theresienstadt to Auschwitz in 1944, but nothing else could be found. Martin stopped writing in 1950. Information found since then reveals that Arthur died in March 1945 in a sub-camp of Dachau.

<u>COPY.</u>

Memo: from Martin Meyer.

Springhill,
MAISEMORE.
Gloucester.

To the Commandant,   28th November, 1946.
Camp for Jewish Detainees,
<u>CYPRUS.</u>

Dear Sir,

   I have recently been informed from The Town Council of Berlin Borough Prenslauer Berg, that my brother ARTHUR MEYER, born Posen on the 4th February 1898 left Berlin in an attempt to get to Palestine by illegal transport in the early part of July this year.

   This brief information has been the first indication that he is alive, which has reached me since September 1939.

   It could be possible that he is in the Camp under your control, and I would be very grateful if you could arrange for some kind of notice to be put up where he might see it if he is at your camp, stating that I am anxious to have news of him. If he is at your camp is it possible for him to have the necessary facilities to communicate with me.

   Your kind and sympathetic interest would be very much appreciated.

      Yours faithfully,

Letter 1 (top left)

RADA ŽIDOVSKÝCH NÁBOŽENSKÝCH OBCÍ V ZEMÍCH ČESKÉ A MORAVSKOSLEZSKÉ

PRAHA V., MAISLOVA 18.

C.

E 4706/Ho.   Praha, dne Jan. 14th, 1947.

Mr. Martin M e y e r,
"Springhill"
Maisemore,
G l o u c e s t e r.,
England.

Dear Sir,

In reply to your letter of Dec.16th,46, we beg to inform
you about the result of our searching for the missing
persons:

Mrs. Helene M e y e r, born on Aug.11th,1895,
Miss Hilde Rita   "   "   Aug.10th,1929,
Steffan   "   "   Jan.9th,1932m
Herbert   "   "   Oct.29th,1937, were deported
from Berlin to the ghetto of Teresin Theresienstadt, on
May 17th,1943 by transport I/12470-92,I-12471-92, I/12472-92,
I/12473-92, from there they were taken to Auschwitz,Poland
on Oct.23rd,1944 by transport Et 205,31,32,33.
Further traces are missing.

Mr. Arthur M e y e r, born on Febr.4th,1898, was deported
to Teresin on May 17th,1943 by transport I/12469-92 and
from there to Auschwitz on Sept.28th,1944 by transport
Ek 676. Further traces missing.

Mrs. Rosa L e w i n, born on July 19th,1876, was sent to
Teresin on Sept.7th,1942 by transport I/6230-60; left for
Poland on May 16th,1944 by transport Sa 1333. All traces
are missing.
The name of Hanna M e y e r is entered only in the cremation-
list of Terezin. She was cremated on Apr.21st,1944, number
of the urn 23433.As in this list only name and date of
cremation without any personal dates such as birth-date etc.
are entered, an identification is impossible.
Unfortunately our investigations about
L e w i n Siegbert,Herta,Meta,Ludvik and Ilse remained
without result. They are not registered on any of our
records.
We are,

yours sincerely:

Council of Jewish Communities
in Bohemia and Moravia

TELEFON 625-41 — MEZIMĚSTSKY 625-41

Letter 2 (top right)

WORLD JEWISH CONGRESS
BRITISH SECTION

SEARCH DEPARTMENT

CONGRESS HOUSE,
55, NEW CAVENDISH STREET,
LONDON, W.1
Telephone: Welbeck 1314 (three lines)
Cables and Telegrams:
Inland: Worldgress, Wesdo, London
Foreign: Worldgress, London

IRS-Meyer-Maisemore.   7th August,1947.

Mr.Martin Meyer,
Springhill,
Maisemore,
Gloucester.
Dear Sir/Madam,

Some time ago you asked us to establish the
address of
          Arthur Meyer in Palestine.

Will you please let us know whether you are by
now in touch with the above mentioned person(s)
or whether you would like us to continue in our
search.

In the latter case, will you kindly complete
the enclosed form and return it to our office.

We remain,

Yours sincerely

SEARCH DEPARTMENT

1 Encl.

P.S. Please note that this refers to your enquiry made to the
Fichier Central Juif(Juedische Zentral-Kartothek)in Geneva whose agenda
we have taken over .

Letter 3 (bottom left)

AMERICAN JOINT DISTRIBUTION COMMITTEE

APO 742a
c/o PM NY, NY

TRACING OFFICE
SUCHABTEILUNG

February 24, 1948.

KRONPRINZENALLEE 247
BERLIN-ZEHLENDORF

Telephones Berlin 76 33 77
76 33 78
76 33 79

Mr. Martin MEYER
~~Miss/Mrs.~~
15th Paragon Clifton
BRISTOL 8, England.

Dear Mr.Meyer:

Re.: Your Inquiry through Deutsches Rotes Kreus, Hamburg
     for MEYER, Arthur, born 4.2.1898 in Poznan,
     last known address: Berlin NO 55, Belforterstr.13

We regret to inform you, that we were unsuccessful in our
attempt to locate the above named.

According to the Deportation Files
          Mr.Arthur MEYER

was/were deported with 54/33927 - 38.East   Transport
on 17.5.1943   to Auschwitz (?)

The above named did not return to ~~his/their~~ former residence
and ~~his/their~~ fate is unknown.

Very sincerely yours,

LARRY LUBETSKY
Tracing Officer
AJDC BERLIN

PLEASE REFER TO:
BEI BEANTW. ANGEBEN:
LL/   hs
file 6115
cc: Deutsches Rotes Kreuz, Hamburg

F.5A

Letter 4 (bottom right)

WORLD JEWISH CONGRESS
EUROPEAN TRACING OFFICE

Ref.   HD/MEYER/BRISTOL
(Please quote in future
correspondence)

CONGRESS HOUSE,
55, NEW CAVENDISH STREET,
LONDON, W.1
Telephone : WEL 0335 (four lines)
Cable Address: Worldgress, London

19th July, 1950

Mr. M. Meyer,
15, The Paragon,
Bristol 8.

Dear Sir,

In reply to your enquiry of June 1949 regarding

the whereabouts of your brother Arthur Meyer,

we regret to inform you that according to informa-

tion from Israel no trace could be found of Mr.

Meyer.

We are sorry not to be able to give you better

news and remain,

Yours sincerely,

EUROPEAN TRACING OFFICE

EPILOGUE

Living Without

Opposite: In 1997, IWM was sent a small container holding human remains from Auschwitz. During the development of IWM's new Holocaust Galleries, the decision was made formally to pass the remains to the UK's Chief Rabbi for burial. The unknown individuals were conveyed to the graveside by a group of survivors and laid to rest at Bushey New Cemetery in North London in 2019. Over a thousand mourners attended.

The Nazis and their collaborators murdered two-thirds of Europe's Jewish population. Six million people. In some parts of Europe, this represented the complete annihilation of entire households, families, communities. Those that remained, the *She'erit Hapleitah* (surviving remnant), were forced to live their lives in the shadow of an incalculable loss. They, and the generations that followed, have each had to confront the aftermath of this destruction in their own way.

In the decades since, wider questions have persisted and developed about how such things were able to happen within the heart of modern Europe. The volume of this interrogation continues to grow – at the time of writing it is one of the most studied periods in history. Those who are drawn to the subject are not just historians, but sociologists, psychologists, psychoanalysts, geographers, philosophers, social theorists – and many more.

Across the world, different terms have emerged to refer to these events. The word 'Holocaust' was not widely used to refer to the Nazis' programme of racial annihilation until the 1970s. Since then there have been ongoing controversies about what it should be used to define. Some countries and communities reject it and have developed their own terms. These conversations continue.

The Neumeyer Family

Hans Neumeyer was deported to the Theresienstadt ghetto and died of tuberculosis in 1944. Vera was deported to Piaski in 1942. It is not known for certain when she was killed, but it is believed she was murdered in Auschwitz-Birkenau. Hans and Vera's children, Raymond and Ruth – who had first come to the UK on the *Kindertransport* – remained in the country for the rest of their lives. Raymond became a geography teacher and lived with his wife and children in St. Albans. Ruth met her husband at teacher training college. They had three children. Her son, Tim, has conducted extensive research into the family's history and donated a substantial collection of documents and photographs to IWM.

Hermine Petschau ⌄

Hermine received a deportation order in July 1942. She was sent to Theresienstadt from Prague on 16 July 1942 and died there on 30 May 1943.

Below: Hermine Petschau in the years before her deportation.

Hala Lichtenstein

Hala recovered in France after liberation. In 1946, she was reunited with her husband Mordecai who had emigrated to Britain after surviving a death march. She learned English by going to the cinema every day and reading. She changed her name to Helen Stone and lived in London with Mordecai and their children.

Leibisch Engelberg

Leibisch and his brother Jozef both survived and returned to Antwerp, Belgium in 1945. Their entire family – including Leibisch's wife and two sons – was murdered. Leibisch was married again in 1947 to fellow survivor Maryla Sonnenblick and they had two daughters, Rita and Tonia. Leibisch never spoke of his experiences.

Oswald Jacobi ⌃

Oswald left Germany for France in 1937 where he began training in hotel management. In summer 1942, Oswald was deported from France to occupied Poland, probably to Auschwitz-Birkenau. He did not survive. His sister Lore went to great efforts to discover the details of his death after the war, but was unable to discover where or when he died.

Above: Oswald Jacobi as a young adult.

The Lasker Family ⌄

Alfons and his wife Edith received a notice of deportation in April 1942. They were sent to the Izbica ghetto in Poland. They were murdered in Izbica in 1942. Their daughter Anita and her sister Renate moved to Britain in 1946 with the help of their sister Marianne. She became a renowned cellist, touring internationally. She married her childhood friend, pianist Peter Wallfisch, in 1952 and they had two children, Raphael and Maya. Anita now lives in London and regularly gives talks about her experiences.

Below: The Lasker family ice-skating with family and friends before the war.

The Imich Family

Stanisław Imich left his family in Kraków to join the Polish Army. He was interned in neutral Romania, then travelled to Paris to re-join the Army. In June 1940 Stanisław left Paris for the UK. He was stationed on the Isle of Bute. Later he discovered that his wife Anna had been killed at Belzec. His son Jan went into hiding, but was discovered and was interned in a series of concentration camps. He was beaten in Mittelbau-Dora for picking up some potato peel and suffered permanent damage to his hearing. Stanisław and Jan were eventually reunited in the UK.

The Trompeter Family

Tauba lived in Mielec, Poland with her family. After the arrival of the Nazis, she and her sister Sara used forged documents to gain employment. Despite these efforts they were captured and together they endured life in the Kraków ghetto and the concentration camps of Płaszów, Auschwitz and Bergen-Belsen. They were liberated in Belsen but Sara died eight days later. Tauba married a British soldier, Max Biber, and moved to the UK.

The Heidenfeld Family

Hortense worked for three years as a domestic cook. She trained as a children's nurse in 1941 and worked tirelessly in hospitals throughout the war. She married Rupert Gordon in 1950 and had two children. After retiring, she kept busy through volunteer work. Her parents, Georg and Stefanie, and younger sister Beate were deported from Riebnig to Theresienstadt. From there, they were taken to Auschwitz-Birkenau and murdered in 1943.

The Haberfeld Family

Alfons was returning to Poland from a business trip in the US when war broke out in 1939. He and his wife returned to the US. Their young daughter Franciszka was stuck in Poland. She was murdered in Belzec. Alfons and Felicia settled in Los Angeles and had a second child. Alfons continued to work in a distillery and the couple founded an organisation for Holocaust survivors.

The Posner Family

Rachel left for Palestine with her husband Akiva and their three children in 1935. Akiva could not bear to be a rabbi for a new community, so became a librarian. Every *Hanukkah*, their grandchildren and great-grandchildren continue to use the same *hanukkiah* that Akiva and Rachel brought with them.

Dora Francken

Dora Francken's husband Oscar had died in 1932. She joined her daughter Ruth in London in 1939. Her son Dr Hans Franken also came to England and married in 1941. Dora became a grandmother in March 1945.

The Wohl Family ∧

Leonhard and Clara Wohl were deported to Auschwitz-Birkenau in February 1943 and murdered. Their children all survived the war. Ilse emigrated first to Uruguay and then Argentina. Eva, Ulli and Kate remained in England. The trunks that Leonard and Clara had packed to emigrate – before the outbreak of war stopped them – reached their daughters in Britain in 1947.

Above: Members of the surviving Wohl family at a party in the 1950s. Ulli is on the left, Eva is third from left.

The Knoller Family >

Freddie went to Belgium, Erich went to the US and Otto illegally went to the Netherlands and then England. Their parents were killed in Auschwitz-Birkenau. Freddie was arrested in France. He survived slave labour at Auschwitz-Monowitz and Mittelbau-Dora. He was reunited with his brothers after the war.

Right: Alfred 'Freddie' Knoller *(centre),* with his brothers Erich *(left)* and Otto *(right),* in Vienna before the war.

The Halpern Family ⌄

Georgy was rounded up from the Izieu children's home where he had been sheltering on 6 April 1944. He was taken to Drancy transit camp and on 13 April he was included on a transport to Auschwitz-Birkenau and gassed on arrival. He was eight years old. His parents, Julius and Serafine, survived the war and moved to Israel. Until their deaths, they never stopped searching for information about their son.

Below: Georgy and his mother Serafine.
Bottom: Julius and Serafine placed this newspaper advert in 1982.

Otto Patriasz

Otto and his wife Margarethe fled to Britain after his release from Dachau in January 1939. He served in the British Army during the war, and Margarethe worked as a domestic servant. They became British citizens in 1947 and Otto changed his name to Oliver Pond. They lived in Oxford for the rest of their lives.

Adolf Blond

Adolf moved to Britain in 1938 with his wife and daughter after the November pogrom. He became a British citizen in 1949.

Walter and Evelyn Finkler

Walter managed to get to England, where his daughter had come on the *Kindertransport* in 1939, but was interned as an 'enemy alien'. In 1946, he trained as a food scientist in Manchester. Evelyn was reunited with her mother in London in the 1940s.

The Koniec Family

Sigmund and Karoline were unable to leave Bratislava. They were held in the Žilina camp in April 1942. Sigmund was deported to Auschwitz-Birkenau and murdered. It is presumed that Karoline was also murdered in Auschwitz-Birkenau. Their two children Dori and Herbi remained in the UK, where they had first arrived on the *Kindertransport*.

Hermann Gutmann

Hermann volunteered to join the British Army, which freed him from the internment camps where he was being kept. He changed his name to Dennis John Goodman. He returned to England from Germany in 1947 after interrogating Nazis about war crimes. He married Lea Apelzon, who was also a survivor, in 1954 and they had three children. He found one grandmother who had survived in hiding. The rest of his family were murdered.

Anna Maria 'Settela' Steinbach

Settela was a Sinti girl from the Netherlands. She was deported from Westerbork to Auschwitz-Birkenau with her family on 19 May 1944. They were taken to the 'Gypsy family camp'. It is believed that nine-year-old Settela was murdered in the gas chambers on 2 August 1944. Her mother, two sisters, two brothers, her aunt, two nephews and niece were also murdered on this day. Only her father survived the war. An image of Settela looking out of the train carriage on her way to Auschwitz has become well known across the world.

Halpern Julius and Sera Fine
request information and details on their son
George Halpern

born October 30, 1935 and taken away by the Germans on April, 1944 from Izieux, France to Auschwitz.

Anyone with information on the above is requested to contact the Halpern family, 27 Rehov Shimkin, Haifa, **Tel. 04-246056.**

The Asscher Family ‹

Dolf Asscher and his family were saved from deportation from Westerbork to Auschwitz-Birkenau by the help of a Dutch lawyer. The lawyer worked with them to concoct a story that their lineage was actually 'Aryan' and not Jewish, because of an invented illegitimate relationship years earlier. After being released from Westerbork they remained in the Netherlands during the war and moved to England in 1947. Dolf — who became known as William — was knighted for his work in medicine. He refused to travel to or through Germany for the rest of his life. The lawyer who helped save the family has been recognised as Righteous Among The Nations by Yad Vashem.

Top: Professor William Asscher.
Above left: Sir William and Lady Asscher and their daughters, Jane and Sophie.

The Hajdu Family ‹

János Hajdu hid with his aunt Iby in Budapest after the German occupation until his father György returned from a labour camp. He was reunited with his mother Livia. After the war, János completed school in Budapest. In November 1956 mother and son escaped from communist Hungary. They built new lives in the United Kingdom, where János changed his name to John. John was awarded an MBE in 2020 for services to Holocaust education.

Left: John Hajdu with his childhood teddy bear at IWM London in 2021.

The Felix Family ‹

Kitty and her mother Lola Rosa survived the Lublin ghetto and a series of camps including Auschwitz-Birkenau. They were the only members of their family not killed. Robert fought in a Polish unit of the Soviet Army and was killed in battle near Stalingrad. Kitty and Lola Rosa moved to England in 1946. Kitty trained as a radiographer – a career she occupied for 50 years – and had two sons and eight grandchildren. She has made several television documentaries and written two memoirs under her married name, Kitty Hart-Moxon. Kitty received an OBE in 2003 for her services to Holocaust education.

Top: Kitty with four of her grandchildren.
Above left: Kitty with her husband Rudi and sons David and Peter.

The Siegel Family ‹

Michael and Mathilde managed to emigrate to Peru in 1940. They remained there for the duration of the war and stayed there after its end. Mathilde taught German in a convent school and in 1953 Michael was able to practise law again, helping German-Jewish refugees in Peru to claim compensation. He received an award for this work. Their children Bea and Peter left Germany on the *Kindertransport* and stayed in Britain for the rest of their lives. They were only able to reunite with their parents years later.

Left: Bea and Peter in England during the war.
Below: Bea with her three sons Jeremy, Danny and Paul.

FURTHER READING

GENERAL HISTORIES
The Final Solution David Cesarani (2016)
The Coming of the Third Reich Richard Evans (2004)
The Third Reich in Power Richard Evans (2005)
The Third Reich at War Richard Evans (2008)
The Years of Persecution Saul Friedländer (2007)
The Years of Extermination Saul Friedländer (2014)

CONTEXT
The Origins of the Final Solution Christopher Browning (2003)
Holocaust Landscapes Tim Cole (2016)
A World Without Jews Alon Confino (2014)
The Holocaust and the Liberal Imagination Tony Kushner (1994)
The Twisted Road to Auschwitz Karl Schleunes (1971)
Histories of the Holocaust Dan Stone (2010)

EINSATZGRUPPEN MASS MURDER
Ordinary Men Christopher Browning (1992)
Masters of Death Richard Rhodes (2002)

POLICY AND GERMAN RESPONSES
Life and Death in the Third Reich Peter Fritzsche (1999)
The Unwritten Order Peter Longerich (2001)
The German War Nicholas Stargardt (2015)

CONCENTRATION CAMPS AND DEATH CAMPS
Belzec, Sobibor, Treblinka Yitzhak Arad (1987)
Into that Darkness Gitta Sereny (1974)
KL Nikolaus Wachsmann (2016)

LIBERATION AND POST-WAR JUSTICE
Reckonings Mary Fulbrook (2018)
East West Street Philippe Sands (2016)
The Liberation of the Camps Dan Stone (2015)

IMAGE LIST

All images © IWM unless otherwise stated. The publishers will be glad to make good in future editions any error or omission brought to their attention.

Guernsey, bl ARCH2021/033 Courtesy Mémorial de la Shoah, tr Documents.26371/MMM Courtesy Peter Urbach, br Documents.15288/D © The Rights Holder; 103 tl HU 139094 Courtesy Timothy Locke, tr HU 139095 Courtesy Timothy Locke, c HU 104333 Courtesy Timothy Locke, bl Documents.13538/A, br Yad Vashem Photo Archive, Jerusalem, 1475_30; 104 t Documents.13618/A, b Documents.13618/B; 105 EPH 2311; 106 t © Klarsfeld Archives (Documents.12883/V), bl © Klarsfeld Archives (Documents.12883/L) br © Klarsfeld Archives (Documents.12883/K); 107 t © Klarsfeld Archives (Documents.12883/W), bl © Klarsfeld Archives (Documents.12883/A), © Klarsfeld Archives (Documents.12883/E); 108 Yad Vashem Photo Archive, Jerusalem, 1379 Socha (Righteous of the Nations file); 109 t USHMM 07631 United States Holocaust Memorial Museum, b Yad Vashem Photo Archive, Jerusalam, Otto Weidt 671 Chapter Eight Yad Vashem Photo Archive, Jerusalem, Plan 2 & Plan 3_Lageplan-des-Kriegsgefangenenlagers-Auschwitz; 113 t EPH 11347, b II-3-K151 Archive of the State Museum at Madjanek; 114 tl Bundesarchiv, Bild 146-2007-0188 / o. Ang., tr HU 74915 © Zentrale Stelle des Landesjustizverwaltungen, c Yad Vashem Photo Archive, Jerusalem, 37389, bl HU 74916 © Zentrale Stelle des Landesjustizverwaltungen, br HU 74917 © Zentrale Stelle des Landesjustizverwaltungen; 115 t II-3-K97 Archive of the State Museum at Madjanek, b II-3-K103 Archive of the State Museum at Madjanek; 117 EPH 2333; 118 Yad Vashem Photo Archive, Jerusalem, 966/4; Chapter Nine 120 Art.IWM ART 17437 7 © The Rights Holder; 123 t UNI 11006, b UNI 7003; 124 Documents.13700/A; 125 Documents.13621/A/A; 126 t CUR 17214, b EPH 2293; 127 MUN 3854; 128 t UNI 11103, bl UNI 12004, br UNI 11097; 130 t Documents.5136/C, cl By Courtesy of Kazerne Dossin-Mechelen, cr EPH 2286, bl EPH 2338; 131 LBY K. 97 / 523; 132 Documents.13281/A; 133 XI-39 Sokolov Museum collection, Vaclav Nemec Archive; 134 Documents.13731/C; 135 tl EPH 1458, tr UNI 11945, bl EPH 7249; Chapter Ten 136 EPH 2708; 138 EPH 10204; 140 COM 718.1; 141 USHMM 42797 United States Holocaust Memorial Museum, courtesy of Anonymous Donor; 142-145 Yad Vashem Photo Archive, Jerusalem, Auschwitz album FA268, 142 FA268 55, 143 FA268 121; 144 FA268 133; 145 FA268 156; 146 © Eva Clarke (Documents.26893/B); 147 t INS 7205, b EPH 2364.2; 148 l EPH 7049, r EPH 7050.1&2; 149 Courtesy the Archival Collection of the State Museum Auschwitz-Birkenau, Oświęcim, PMO_nr neg 280, 281, 282, 283; 150-151 © The artist (Art.IWM ART 16666); Chapter Eleven 152 BU 3766; 154 BU 5471; 155 BU 6365; 156 t © The rights holder (HU 59502A), b The Boys Courtesy 45 Aid Society; 158 t BU 7805, bl EPH 10511, br EPH 10142; 159 EPH 5546; 160-161 Art.ILN: 2304 Courtesy Mary Evans Picture Library; Chapter Twelve 162 HU 59545; 164 Courtesy USA Government (Art.IWM PST 8350); 165 t-b BU 9711, BU 9700, USHMM 1922 United States Holocaust Memorial Museum Collection, Gift of Sheila C. Johnson, (TNA RW 2/1) Carmen Mory © The National Archives; 166 t USHMM 49679 United States Holocaust Memorial Museum, courtesy of Stuart McKeever, b USHMM 10375 United States Holocaust Memorial Museum, courtesy of Harry S. Truman Library; 167 t Documents.2074/A, b Art.IWM ART 17451 13 & Art.IWM ART 17451 4 Courtesy dmg media licensing; 168 Art.IWM ART 16518 24 © The Rights Holder; 169 t Art.IWM ART 16518 21, b Art.IWM ART 16518 35 © The Rights Holder; 170 USHMM 78270 United States Holocaust Memorial Museum, courtesy of Hadassah Bimko Rosensaft; 171 t EA 65392, bl BU 7017, br BU 7016; 172 514694008 Bettmann via Getty Images; 173 t USHMM 64910 United States Holocaust Memorial Museum, courtesy of the Sutzkever Family, c USHMM 43039 United States Holocaust Memorial Museum, courtesy of National Archives and Records Administration, College Park, b USHMM footage no. 2001.358.1 United States Holocaust Memorial Museum; 174 Bundesarchiv, Bild 183-V00274 / o. Ang.; 175 l EPH 9329, r Art.IWM PST 9056; 176 Documents.6573/H; 177 tl Documents.6573/P, tr Documents.6573/L Courtesy World Jewish Congress, bl Documents.6573/M Courtesy American Jewish Joint Distribution Committee, Inc (JDC), br Documents.6573/O Courtesy World Jewish Congress; Epilogue 178 Courtesy Blake Ezra Photography; 180 l 8068.1.2 © Estate of Oswald Jacobi, r Documents.13538/B; 181 HU 139999 © The rights holder; 182 t Pro 43 IMG 3874 Courtesy Peter Urbach, b HU 140012 © The estate of Freddie Knoller; 183 t © Klarsfeld Archives (Documents.12883 K), b © Klarsfeld Archives (Documents.12883 X); 184 tl & tr Courtesy the Asscher Family, bl IWM 2021 030 0021; 185 tl & tr Courtesy the Felix Family, bl & br Courtesy the Siegel Family.

ACKNOWLEDGEMENTS

This book is based on the content of IWM London's Holocaust Galleries, and on the research conducted by the author in his role as Head of Content for IWM London's Holocaust Galleries project team. The historical content of the galleries – and, by extension, of this book – evolved in consultation with the following advisory board:

Professor Dan Stone (Chair)
Ben Barkow
Professor Tim Cole
Professor Tony Kushner
Professor Richard Overy
Paul Salmons
Dr Zoe Waxman
and with the galleries' content team, Jessica Talarico (curator and exhibition manager), Lucy May Maxwell (curator) and Lauren Willmott (curator).

IWM would like to thank those who have kindly provided their advice, expertise and assistance, including Professor Robert Eaglestone, Tania Gessi, Dr Stefan Hördler, Rabbi Nicky Liss, Professor Philippe Sands, Professor Rainer Schulze and Professor Nik Wachsmann. IWM is grateful to all our Holocaust Galleries supporters including Pears Foundation, Garfield Weston Foundation, The Wolfson Foundation, and The National Lottery Heritage Fund.

We would also like to thank those people, families and community groups who assisted in the development of the project and whose objects, images and stories appear in the galleries and this book, as well as the museums and archives that have helped us to tell their stories.

Further thanks are due to Suzanne Bardgett, Ann Carter, Professor David Cesarani, Rebecca Derine, Rachel Donnelly, James Taylor and Gary Shelley of Casson Mann.
Finally, thanks to Madeleine James of IWM Publishing.

ABOUT THE AUTHOR

James Bulgin is Head of Content for the new Holocaust Galleries at Imperial War Museums. He started work on the project in 2016. Before joining IWM James worked as a commercial theatre producer and director, with work in the West End and on national tour. He is currently completing a PhD under the Crosslands scholarship at Royal Holloway College, University of London, on ideas of apocalypse in Holocaust and Cold War history. His academic research focuses on issues of representation in Holocaust literature and film, and he has spoken at conferences in the UK, Israel and Germany.

INDEX

Page numbers in **bold** refer to illustration captions